Getting Better Faster

Getting Better Faster

A Clinician's Guide to Intensive Treatment for Youth with OCD

AVITAL FALK, PHD

SHANNON BENNETT, PHD

MICHELLE ROZENMAN, PHD

JUSTIN MOHATT, MD

R. LINDSEY BERGMAN, PHD

OXFORD
UNIVERSITY PRESS

OXFORD
UNIVERSITY PRESS

Oxford University Press is a department of the University of Oxford. It furthers
the University's objective of excellence in research, scholarship, and education
by publishing worldwide. Oxford is a registered trade mark of Oxford University
Press in the UK and certain other countries.

Published in the United States of America by Oxford University Press
198 Madison Avenue, New York, NY 10016, United States of America.

© Oxford University Press 2023

Library of Congress Cataloging-in-Publication Data
Names: Falk, Avital, author. | Bennett, Shannon M., author. |
Rozenman, Michelle, author. | Mohatt, Justin, author. | Bergman, R. Lindsey, author.
Title: Getting better faster : a clinician's guide to intensive treatment for youth with OCD /
Avital Falk, Shannon Bennett, Michelle Rozenman, Justin Mohatt, R. Lindsey Bergman.
Description: New York, NY : Oxford University Press, [2023] |
Includes bibliographical references.
Identifiers: LCCN 2022027595 (print) | LCCN 2022027596 (ebook) |
ISBN 9780197670149 (paperback) | ISBN 9780197670156 (epub) | ISBN 9780197670170
Subjects: LCSH: Obsessive-compulsive disorder in children—Treatment. | Intensive psychot-herapy.
Classification: LCC RJ506.O25 F35 2022 (print) | LCC RJ506.O25 (ebook) |
DDC 618.92/85227—dc23/eng/20220816
LC record available at https://lccn.loc.gov/2022027595
LC ebook record available at https://lccn.loc.gov/2022027596

DOI: 10.1093/med-psych/9780197670149.001.0001

9 8 7 6 5 4 3 2 1

Printed by Marquis, Canada

TABLE OF CONTENTS

The forms and worksheets provided in Getting Better Faster can also be accessed online by searching for this book's title on the Oxford Academic platform, at academic.oup.com.

INTRODUCTION AND ACKNOWLEDGMENTS

Intensive treatment options for youth with obsessive compulsive disorder (OCD) are growing: The number and type of programs are increasing, and more families are interested in them. We wrote this guidebook based on our collective experiences launching and running intensive treatment programs across a number of locations and settings. Some of the elements of this book are and have been used in other areas. The acronyms in the treatment chapters and the Appendix (TINTED [Telling the future, Interpreting ambiguity, Negative focus, Taking blame, Exaggerating, predicting Disaster] and SOLVE [State the problem, Options, Look closely, Vote, Evaluate]) have been developed and used by Avital Falk and colleagues at Weill Cornell Medicine/New York Presbyterian Hospital in clinical materials and within an app-based program. The Home-Based Symptom Assessment that is included in the Appendix was developed by R. Lindsey Bergman and Michelle Rozenman in 2014.

As we discuss in several places of this guidebook, it takes a village to start, maintain, and expand programs for youth with OCD. We want to acknowledge and thank our many colleagues at our current and past institutions, without whom our work could not exist. In addition to our colleagues, we can't stress the importance of trainee therapists enough. Our trainees create an incredible atmosphere that our patients and families love, and many of our former trainees have gone on to create their own programs across the country. Even among this group of authors, some of us started out as trainees of others, and we are testament to the strong mentor–trainee relationship and how a passion for treating OCD in an intensive setting can grow in that context. Finally, we want to thank the many, many families, children, and adolescents that we have worked with over the years. The willingness of these kids, teens, and their families to take the risk of embarking on treatment journeys have provided us with more passion for our work than we can convey, and we are in awe of these young people for fighting OCD. As our prior and current patients know, the treatment process is collaborative and a team effort: We are so appreciative of each person with whom we have worked. While our experiences have been shaped by our colleagues, trainees, and patients, it is important to note that examples in this guidebook are not based on specific individual people or examples, and any resemblance is pure coincidence.

Throughout this book, we describe treatment and practice elements. At the time of the writing of this book, these are the best practices. Simultaneously, just as intensive programs are expanding, the research literature constantly reports ongoing new developments in both research and clinical practice. We recognize that, as time passes, there may be advancements that supplement or substitute what we have described here.

Thank you for reading: We hope you find the work we describe as fulfilling and rewarding as we do!

Avital Falk

Shannon Bennett

Michelle Rozenman

Justin Mohatt

R. Lindsey Bergman

Why Do We Need Intensive Treatment for OCD?

Obsessive compulsive disorder (OCD) is characterized by obsessions, which include intrusive thoughts, images, or impulses that cause discomfort and distress, and/or compulsions, which are compensatory behaviors, habits, routines, or rituals performed in an attempt to achieve temporary relief from discomfort. We have excellent evidence-based therapies for OCD, described further in this chapter, which are typically delivered in an outpatient setting with one, or at most two, sessions, scheduled each week. *Intensive treatment* takes the traditional elements of the established evidence-based treatments and delivers them with higher frequency. This may be recommended because symptoms are too severe to address in less intensive treatment or to condense treatment into a shorter time period. There is strong research support indicating that intensive treatment works as well as traditional weekly interventions and may have additional qualitative benefits.

There are special populations who may benefit from an intensive treatment model. Children and adolescents who are partial responders or nonresponders to medication or to previous outpatient treatment may have greater success in a treatment where they have daily contact with a therapist. The accelerated momentum that an intensive treatment program offers is helpful for patients who have difficulty resisting OCD symptoms or difficulty practicing suggested interventions, such as exposure exercises, on their own between sessions. Similarly, for patients with symptoms that interfere with engagement in day-to-day activities or school attendance, an intensive treatment program provides the opportunity to complete treatment and improve functioning in a shorter period of time. The accelerated nature of intensive treatment might prevent a child from needing a higher level of care, repeating a grade, or switching a school setting. Finally, when an individual is discharged from an inpatient unit, residential treatment, or partial hospitalization program, weekly treatment may not be a sufficient next level of care. Instead, an intensive treatment program may provide a more gradual decrease in the amount of therapy time and support for the patient and their family, allowing for a later seamless transition to weekly outpatient care.

Intensive treatment programs can be beneficial for a broad range of individuals and symptom presentations. The term "intensive" often implies that the treatment is for high levels of symptom severity. Indeed, many children and adolescents who experience severe OCD benefit from intensive treatment. However, the intensive treatment approach may expedite the pace of treatment and make treatment more accessible to patients with mild-to-moderate symptoms as well. Evidence-based care can be challenging to find, even for families who are aware of gold standard treatment strategies. There is a dearth of qualified mental health providers in many areas, leaving large populations facing the challenge of how to access care. Evidence-based outpatient treatment is often not an option if there is no local clinician who can provide specialized services. For patients who do not have access to appropriate evidence-based care, an intensive treatment program can provide the opportunity to spend as few as days or weeks in one place and receive a full course of treatment. Even among those who *do* live in areas that have providers with appropriate expertise, some families may opt to participate in intensive treatment programs because a treatment course can be completed over a school break or vacation period when families have the time to fully commit.

The level of detail provided in this chapter, and in this guidebook, on the established treatments for OCD assumes some previous experience and familiarity with gold standard treatments for OCD, particularly exposure and response prevention (ERP). Thus, a clinician new to OCD treatment who is looking for a step-by-step guide on how to implement ERP should consult other texts (e.g., Franklin et al., 2019; Piacentini et al., 2007). This guidebook is an appropriate reference for clinicians, scholars, administrators, or other professionals with experience in the treatment of OCD who are interested in implementing this treatment in a condensed or intensive format.

HOW TO USE THIS GUIDEBOOK

Section I: This section is designed to provide context and background for, and benefits of, the intensive treatment model. This chapter, Chapter 1, provides a review of pediatric OCD and describes the nonintensive, evidence-based treatment approaches for this condition, providing the foundation and context for the intensive treatment model. In Chapter 2, we describe the research support for the intensive treatment model, and in Chapter 3, we detail the clinical benefits of intensive treatment.

Section II: In Chapters 4 through 7, we offer a comprehensive guide for program implementation and development, as well as specific instruction on delivering treatment strategies in an intensive modality. We cover the range and possibilities for program structures (Chapter 4), barriers and logistics of program implementation (Chapter 5), staffing and training models

(Chapter 6), and a discussion of treatment pathways that patients
may travel (Chapter 7).

Section III: The last section provides clinical descriptions of and materials for
the elements of intensive cognitive behavioral therapy (CBT) and
ERP and discusses the unique challenges and clinical applications
of each core treatment element within the intensive treatment
framework.

OBSESSIVE COMPULSIVE DISORDER: AN OVERVIEW

The lifetime prevalence of OCD is estimated to be around 2%–3% (Kessler et al.,
2005), and the disorder typically follows a chronic course (Skoog & Skoog, 1999).
Prevalence rates are around 1%–2% in pediatric populations (Flament et al.,
1988). OCD is among the most disabling of psychiatric and medical conditions
without adequate intervention and puts youth at risk for other psychiatric and
behavioral health problems (Murray & Lopez, 1996). OCD has a bimodal age
of onset, with the first vulnerable period occurring around the time of puberty
(roughly age 10–12) and the second occurring around the transition from adolescence to emerging adulthood (age 18–23) (Anholt et al., 2014; Geller, 2006).

There is a wide range of OCD symptom presentations in children and
adolescents. For some, the content of obsessions and compulsions can be singular and cluster around one theme. Other patients present with a variety of different types of obsessions and compulsions across multiple themes. Obsessions
tend to be unrealistic, irrational, or superstitious in nature and are typically not
simply excessive worries about real-life stressors or everyday events. A compulsion may be related to the content of an obsession (e.g., washing hands when
concerned about germs or contamination) but is out of proportion to the reality
of the situation (e.g., washing hands 10 to 20 times successively). Often, the connection between an obsession and a compulsion is unrealistic or may not appear
to be clearly linked (e.g., avoiding walking over a crack in the street to prevent
something bad from happening to a loved one; counting up to a certain number
after experiencing an intrusive thought about safety). There are several common
content categories of obsessions and compulsions (see Appendix Table A.1), but
the specific content, number, and combination of obsessions and compulsions
are unique to each affected individual. The common content of obsessions and
compulsions may include contamination from germs or getting sick; a strong
need for things to be even or in a particular order; unwanted thoughts that are
sexual, violent, or religious in nature; repetitive checking or excessive reassurance seeking; and irrational avoidance of neutral stimuli that the patient fears may
cause harm or bad luck. Although there are unlimited expressions of OCD symp-
tomatology, the fictional examples below describe two fairly typical presentations.

Marcus is a 10-year-old male with obsessions related to contamination from
germs and a fear of getting sick, especially throwing up. He avoids touching

public doorknobs with his hands and avoids using public restrooms whenever possible for fear of contamination from germs. He washes his hands
excessively throughout the day, making sure to use five pumps of soap because he feels this is a lucky number, and he rinses for at least a count of 100.
If he loses count while rinsing, he begins again, which often ends up taking
a long time. He sometimes asks his parents to pick things up or open doors
for him so that he does not have to wash again if he touches something he
feels is "germy." He also often eats a different meal from the rest of the family
because he fears certain foods may cause him to vomit.

Jill is a 14-year-old female who has intrusive, unwanted, thoughts of
hurting herself or someone else unintentionally. She has intrusive images of
someone tripping over something she has dropped and getting hurt. In response to these thoughts and images, she makes sure to be meticulously neat
and repeatedly checks the floor and area around her at school and at home to
make sure she hasn't dropped something or left something out of place that
could cause harm to someone else. When she walks to school in the morning,
she sometimes has to return home to make sure she has remembered to pick
everything up off the floor in her room, or she stops and retraces her steps
to make sure that she didn't drop something and thus is often late to school.
She also checks her homework responses 10 times to ensure she has not for-
gotten to answer something or made a mistake, and she erases and rewrites
certain words or letters until they look perfect to her.

Many people have intrusive thoughts or habits that do not cause interference
in daily life. Diagnostic criteria for OCD include the presence of obsessions and/
or compulsions, significant time spent engaging with or responding to obsessions
and compulsions, and interference or impact on day-to-day life due to OCD. In the
fifth edition of the *Diagnostic and Statistical Manual of Mental Disorders* (*DSM-5*;
American Psychiatric Association, 2013), OCD was moved out of the category of
anxiety disorders and reassigned to its own category, now called "obsessive compulsive and related disorders" (OCRDs). This change represents decades of research that may support OCD as biologically and phenomenologically distinct
from non-OCD anxiety disorders (Abramowitz & Ryan, 2014; Stein et al., 2014).

NONINTENSIVE INTERVENTION FOR OCD

There are strong evidence-based interventions for OCD. Several studies have
shown that CBT and pharmacotherapy with selective serotonin reuptake
inhibitors (SSRIs) to be efficacious and effective interventions for pediatric OCD;
however, nearly 50% of children receiving both CBT and sertraline, an SSRI, did
not meet criteria for clinical remission in the most rigorous randomized control
trial of these interventions (POTS Team, 2004). As such, substantial research and
clinical efforts strive to improve extant interventions for pediatric OCD, including
the delivery of treatment in an intensive or condensed format.

The gold standard nonpharmacological treatment for OCD is a form of CBT that focuses on ERP. The core of ERP includes supporting patients in facing the content of their fears or obsessions without engaging in compulsive behaviors, rituals, or avoidance. ERP is used in tandem with other CBT interventions, like cognitive restructuring, mindfulness, problem solving and planning, and education about anxiety, OCD, and the rationale behind exposure therapy. Because ERP is the backbone of the intensive treatment modality, from here on, we use the term ERP when describing the treatment, though we acknowledge and will go into greater depth about the other CBT skills that are used in the course of treatment. A reward system can be used to support initial and continued practice of exposure exercises with patients who need additional motivation. Moreover, identified support people, such as parents, teachers, siblings, and other trusted peers or adults, can help patients engage in exposures outside of the treatment session. Section III of this guidebook details these interventions, and the Appendix provides sample worksheets for the different skills.

In the case of Marcus described previously in this chapter, ERP would focus on systematically touching things in the environment perceived as "germy," including doorknobs and toilets, while simultaneously resisting the urge to engage in the full washing ritual with the ultimate goal of eradicating all OCD-related washing. Work with his parents would include reducing OCD related accommodation (i.e., refraining from picking things up for Marcus or cooking him separate meals). Additional treatment techniques with Marcus might include cognitive restructuring strategies to consider the true likelihood of getting sick or throwing up based on past experiences or sheer probability. For Jill, ERP would include resisting urges to retrace steps or check the areas around her for dropped belongings, as well as, later in treatment, intentionally leaving objects scattered around her. Additional exposure exercises would focus on compulsions related to schoolwork. She could use mindfulness strategies to bring awareness to her intrusive thoughts without responding to them and to observe her anxiety as it subsequently rises and falls. For both Marcus and Jill, psychoeducation about OCD and understanding the rationale and theory behind ERP early on in treatment will help them understand the symptoms they are experiencing and ideally also build motivation to participate in treatment. More examples and considerations for these treatment components are detailed in Section III of this guidebook.

Treatment of OCD often includes medication in addition to ERP. In fact, research indicated that while both ERP and SSRIs are effective treatments for OCD, for youth with moderate-to-severe symptoms, the combination of an SSRI and ERP is significantly more effective than either alone (POTS Team, 2004). Children and adolescents with mild OCD symptoms, and younger children without prior treatment history, may be offered ERP alone, but any youth with moderate-to-severe symptoms should be offered combination treatment with an SSRI and ERP in order to provide the strongest evidence-based care. While SSRIs and ERP have been found effective for treating children and adolescents with OCD, there remain a substantial percentage of patients who either do not respond or have an inadequate response to standard treatments (POTS Team, 2004). We discuss the role of medications more thoroughly in Chapter 8.

There are a variety of additional strategies to address the symptoms in treatment-refractory patients; these strategies vary from alternative medications and medication augmentation strategies to more complicated and invasive procedures for the most severely affected patients. Options for these most severely affected patients include ablative neurosurgery, deep brain stimulation, focused ultrasound, and gamma knife treatment. More recently, repetitive transcranial magnetic stimulation (rTMS) was approved by the Food and Drug Administration (FDA) for the treatment of adults with OCD in combination with CBT. This is not yet approved for use in children and adolescents. At present, the evidence base for all these advanced medical strategies remains nonexistent for children and adolescents. While the details of these interventions are beyond the scope of this book, it is important to be aware of them, as a number of patients presenting for intensive ERP are likely to have exhausted typical evidence-based treatments and may present with questions regarding these options.

In addition to the various treatments available to patients with OCD, there is also a continuum of care for youth with OCD. This book focuses largely on intensive treatment in an outpatient setting, but there are additional levels of care for patients who require even more intensive services or a more restricted setting for safety and containment. Partial hospital programs (PHPs) provide the next step up in care from intensive treatment in an outpatient setting and provide patients with treatment for multiple hours a day on a daily basis, while still allowing them to sleep at home. While some intensive treatment programs similarly offer multiple hours of intervention daily, PHPs support individuals with a level of symptom impairment or interference that is higher than that of an intensive outpatient program, often close to that required for inpatient care. The hours are often throughout the school day, rather than after school or during a scheduled break, reflecting that level of impairment. Patients who do not show improvement despite application of evidence-based treatments in outpatient or PHP settings may require placement in a specialized residential facility. These facilities can provide highly specialized care around the clock, but often are geographically far from home and can be financially prohibitive for patients without residential coverage through their health plans. Finally, at times patients with OCD have such severe impairment from their OCD (e.g., not eating, not caring for basic needs) or present with acute safety concerns (e.g., aggression or suicidality) and require inpatient treatment. Most inpatient treatment is not specialized for OCD, however, and the treatment focus is often on crisis stabilization.

THE ROLE OF INTENSIVE TREATMENT

Intensive treatment models grew out of a need to make evidence-based treatment for OCD more accessible and effective for all patients who need it. OCD is a complicated and debilitating disorder with well-established evidence-based treatments, but these treatments often are not effective or not available for eve-ryone, and patients need alternatives. Intensive or condensed treatment programs for OCD have grown increasingly common and popular over the last 10–15 years. There are several advantages to an intensive course of ERP and asso-ciated interventions that are described in detail throughout this book. Research supported that intensive ERP is as effective as weekly ERP, and the relief from the symptoms of OCD is often achieved in a shorter period of time in an inten-sive treatment program. Moreover, ERP works best when repeated and practiced often. The structure of intensive treatment allows the therapist to engage a pa-tient at several time points throughout the week, reinforcing the principles and active ingredients of the treatment and decreasing the time in between sessions when patients may have a harder time using treatment strategies on their own. Therapists can help patients move more assertively through necessary exposure exercises and take more planned "risks" in their selection of challenging exposures because the longer session duration in an intensive program allows the patient to spend more time engaging with the exposure, processing the emotions and ex-perience, and beginning to recover from whatever level of distress was experi-enced before leaving the session. Intensive programs that offer a group therapy component also provide embedded social support and may decrease shame and stigma by allowing youth and families to meet others with similar experiences of OCD. There is no standard structure or schedule that defines intensive treatment. Instead, there are a variety of ways that treatment sessions can be made longer in duration and occur more frequently in a given week. We outline a number of dif-ferent approaches and example schedules in Chapter 4.

CHAPTER 1 TAKE-HOME POINTS

- OCD is characterized by obsessions, which include intrusive thoughts, images, or impulses that cause discomfort and distress, and/or compulsions, which are compensatory behaviors, habits, routines, or rituals performed to achieve temporary relief.
- Intensive treatment takes the traditional elements of evidence-based treatments and delivers them with higher frequency.
- There is strong research support indicating that intensive treatment works as well as traditional weekly interventions and may have additional qualitative benefits.
- Intensive treatments can help when symptoms are too severe to address in less intensive treatment *or* to condense treatment into a shorter period of time even for mild or moderate cases.
- Intensive treatment models grew out of a need to make evidence-based treatment for OCD more accessible and effective for all patients who need it.

Evidence for Intensive Treatment Programs

RESEARCH SUPPORT FOR INTENSIVE TREATMENT

There is a strong and compelling evidence base that supports cognitive behavior therapy (CBT) and exposure and response prevention (ERP) as the front-line psychosocial treatment for obsessive compulsive disorder (OCD; Rosa-Alcázar et al., 2008), and in recent years, there has been an increased focus on optimizing the implementation of these treatments. As discussed in Chapter 1, while original ERP treatment protocols were based on a format of "one session per week," there is ample and growing support for providing OCD treatment in a more intensive manner, which we in depth here. Intensive treatment tends to span 3 to 15 hours a week and can provide the same skills and intervention in a condensed time period or the same treatment at a higher "dose" or intensity. Intensive treatments are gaining popularity, are as effective as weekly therapy, can be flexibly applied, and may have unique benefits for special populations who are not be able to commit to the length of time required for a full course of weekly treatment, who are stepping down from a higher (i.e., inpatient, residential) level of care, or who have previously failed traditional once-weekly outpatient treatment. In this chapter, we provide a brief history and review of intensive treatment models and present the qualitative and quantitative benefits of these models for youth with OCD.

CLINICAL TRIALS

The first mention of intensive treatment models pre-dates the first studies examining them. Intensive treatments were described first in the 1980s as a clinical service provided within research studies on other OCD-related topics (Cottraux et al., 1984; Jenike, 1990; Steketee, 1993). At that time, intensive treatment was defined as five 90-minute sessions per week over 4 to 8 weeks using ERP. This approach is not very different from many of the current models.

Despite being used clinically as early as the 1980s, the first research study focusing specifically on the efficacy of intensive treatment protocols for youth was not published until 1998. This was a study comparing OCD-affected children who received intensive treatment versus those receiving weekly treatment, both treatments consisting of CBT and ERP, and showed a positive response in both groups (Franklin et al., 1998). This study was supported about a decade later by a full randomized control trial, which similarly supported that both intensive and weekly CBT are efficacious delivery models for youth with OCD (Storch, Geffken, et al., 2007). The most recent review of research trials to date consists of a meta-analysis of 17 trials across adults and children and 646 participants, and showed large pre- to post-intervention effect sizes of intensive treatment (Jónsson et al., 2015). This meta-analysis, which synthesized findings across the literature, indicated that the intensive format is an acceptable manner to administer CBT for OCD. Beyond these research trials, the literature describing the qualitative and quantitative benefits of intensive treatment has grown exponentially, indicating the attention and reception that these treatments have received (see Appendix Table A.2).

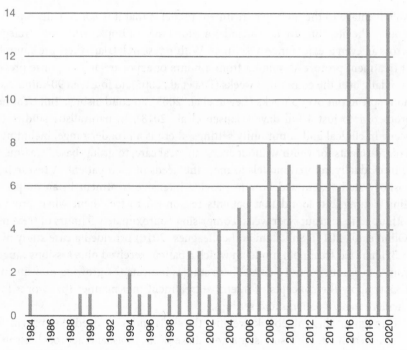

Number of publications on PsycInfo Database using or examining intensive treatment by year.

In addition to clinical trials that directly compare intensive treatment with traditional weekly outpatient treatment models, preliminary data support that neurobiological changes that parallel symptom reduction in OCD treatment for adults occur within a condensed time period. While this work has not yet been replicated in youth, these studies indicated that changes in response to rapid treatment influence, not only behavior (e.g., decreasing avoidance), but also the neurobiological processes proposed to underlie OCD. In adult studies using a variety of methods, including positron emission tomography (PET) scans (Saxena et al., 2009), magnetic resonance spectroscopic imaging (MRSI; O'Neill et al., 2013), and functional magnetic resonance imaging (fMRI) studies (Feusner et al., 2015, Moody et al., 2017 and Reggente et al., 2018) to examine brief and intensive interventions, there is strong evidence that these short-term treatments yielded neurobiological changes. Given that these studies were exclusively in adults, further research in youth is warranted to explore the biological changes in a developing brain that accompany the observed behavioral results of intensive treatments. Moreover, these changes provide initial evidence that intensive treatment for OCD may alter the processes that underlie this disorder, further increasing confidence that an intensive treatment approach is efficacious.

WHAT DOES "INTENSIVE TREATMENT" LOOK LIKE?

An advantage to the intensive treatment model is that it is *not* actually one rigid model! The literature to date includes a wide range of implementation strategies, across an even greater range of settings. Within research trials, there are a number of treatment protocols, ranging from 2 hours of exposure and response prevention daily over the course of 3 weeks (Foa et al., 2005), to fourteen 90-minute sessions spread out over 3 weeks (Lewin et al., 2005), to condensing a full treatment protocol into just 4 full days (Hansen et al., 2018). In naturalistic studies that occur in clinical and community settings, there is a broader range, including 5-day treatments for youth without access to local care, to group-based treatments, to individually tailored models to meet the needs of each patient. A research repository study examined how to provide intensive treatment in an outpatient clinic setting and found that patients responded to treatment when provided with up to four groups per week, comprising approximately 9 hours of treatment (Olino et al., 2011). Shikatani and colleagues (2016) provided a case study of an individualized treatment model in which a patient received nine sessions ranging from 2 to 4 hours over 11 days. These studies indicate the growing movement to flexibly apply the concepts of intensive treatment in a manner that works for a broader range of patients and settings.

Throughout this guidebook, we offer the skills and tools needed to provide intensive treatment. We also discuss how these skills, tools, and approaches can be used across a number of settings, including community clinics, training-based clinics, private practices, and research settings. Additionally, we provide information about some relative strengths and challenges between these various settings and structures so that clinicians can weigh their options and decide which type of intensive setting and treatment might best fit their skills, availability, and patient population.

CHAPTER 2 TAKE-HOME POINTS

- While original treatment protocols for OCD were based on an outpatient format of one session per week, there is ample and growing support for providing OCD treatment in a more intensive manner.
- An advantage to the intensive treatment model is that it is not actually one rigid model. There are many ways to apply the model.
- Intensive treatment tends to span 3 to 15 hours a week and can provide the same skills and intervention in a condensed time period or the same treatment at a higher dose or intensity.
- Intensive treatments are gaining popularity, are as effective as weekly therapy, can be flexibly applied, and may have unique benefits for special populations.
- The literature describing the qualitative and quantitative benefits of intensive treatment has grown exponentially.

Clinical Benefits of Intensive Pediatric OCD Treatment Models

In this chapter, we review the practical benefits of intensive treatment for pediatric obsessive compulsive disorder (OCD), as well as some important pragmatic issues for families and clinicians to consider when deciding whether an intensive level of care is appropriate. We begin with a discussion of the advantages of an intensive treatment setting. We then review the range of settings in which an intensive approach might be well suited, including considerations for therapists when developing components of the intensive treatment setting. We follow with a description of the ideal target population for intensive treatment of pediatric OCD, as well as a description of individuals for whom the intensive level of care may and may not be appropriate. The chapter concludes with important information for the clinician to discuss and agree on with youth and family prior to initiating intensive treatment for pediatric OCD.

ADVANTAGES OF INTENSIVE TREATMENT

There are several distinct advantages of intensive treatment as compared to typical once-weekly outpatient treatment for children and adolescents. The first and most obvious is an increased number of intervention hours in a given week. This extra time spent may allow for faster traction on symptom reduction, which becomes particularly important in later stages of treatment when gains in the therapy room are expected to generalize out of session into the patient's day-to-day life. The potential for greater gains and symptom reduction in a shorter period of time may also decrease functional impairment more quickly, which allows patients to return to age-appropriate and expected activities (e.g., school, extracurriculars, spending time with friends). Speed of functional improvement may also influence the speed at which functioning for other family members improves (e.g., parent returns to work more quickly). Similarly, it may reduce secondary depressive symptoms more quickly when patients experience mood symptoms related to their OCD (e.g., hopelessness, guilt, or concerns that symptoms will not remit).

An additional important advantage of intensive treatment over once-weekly outpatient treatment is that some patients may be able to complete the majority of treatment over a winter/summer break and resume school on the same timeline as their peers; this may be especially true for patients in the mild-to-moderate symptom range who are motivated for and compliant with treatment.

It may be difficult to effectively manage time in a once-weekly outpatient therapy session if the provider needs to address both OCD symptoms and other clinical issues. In contrast, intensive treatment can provide the means to systematically address other issues without compromising or disrupting the treatment of OCD. Examples of common problems that arise and must be addressed in treatment may include, but are not limited to, diagnostic comorbidity, parent/family intervention as part of OCD treatment, and/or unexpected issues such as an increase in suicidal ideation or behavior. More intervention hours and more frequent face time per week allow therapists to better and more effectively manage patient safety. This may be particularly true for patients who experience suicidal ideation and/or are at risk for self-harm secondary to distress from OCD symptoms, have difficulties with medication compliance and/or side effects, and/or have other medical concerns that may occur as a function of OCD symptoms (e.g., handwashing to the point of lesions, dietary restrictions as a result of fears of contamination or vomiting). If embedded in a multidisciplinary setting such as a hospital, an intensive program may comprise a team of providers, including psychiatrists, psychologists, and other services (e.g., nutrition, social work). The team approach may be better suited to managing certain types of symptoms (e.g., food contamination) or comorbidities together, as compared to a single provider pursuing collateral contacts or relationships outside of the core network (e.g., private practice outpatient therapist who needs to identify a child psychiatrist with specialty training in OCD treatment for collaboration).

The condensed schedule of intensive treatment may provide a context in which families can more rapidly learn key lessons about managing pediatric OCD. For example, a patient may learn more quickly that exposure-based treatment can be effective, and that high levels of distress during exposures (and, ultimately, in their daily life) are tolerable for prolonged periods of time. In turn, this may increase patients' motivation to participate in sessions and complete assigned between-session practices. Similarly, parents may learn that they can tolerate their child's distress without engaging in accommodation and more quickly reduce accommodation under the provider's guidance. The family may also feel more broadly supported during the treatment course, which again may increase motivation to participate.

Finally, although not necessary for intensive treatment to be successful, many intensive programs involve group work, which can be a significant benefit in regard to motivation and social support. While once-weekly outpatient exposure and response prevention (ERP) in a group format can be successful, balancing between group management and providing personalized treatment for each patient/family may be difficult. It is our collective experience that intensive treatment that involves at least some time spent doing group work (e.g., group exposures, group mindfulness exercises, parenting support groups) results in patients and parents feeling connected and less alone. It also normalizes the treatment experience. The impact of the group on individual patients and families is striking. The social milieu in which patients encourage one another to complete difficult exposures and the manner in which families support each other as they support their own children can be powerful tools to further increase compliance and motivation, and subsequent success, in treatment.

INTENSIVE TREATMENT SETTINGS AND RECOMMENDATIONS

The research literature suggests that intensive treatment can be conducted across a wide variety of settings. Papers published on intensive treatments (see Chapter 2 and Appendix Table A.2) provide strong evidence that intensive treatment can be conducted in a wide range of settings (e.g., hospital, community clinic, and private practice), and that evidence-based intensive treatment can be helpful regardless of the setting in which it is embedded. Moreover, intensive treatment can encompass a range of hours per day/week and range of weeks. In this context, our recommendations for therapists who are thinking about developing an intensive treatment program for pediatric OCD is that providers focus less on the specific setting in which treatment might occur and more on specific considerations that can increase the likelihood that treatment will be successful. We detail each of these considerations below and encourage therapists to consider these carefully prior to starting an intensive treatment program, again, regardless of the setting in which they may be embedded.

1. *Pharmacotherapy.* As indicated in Chapter 1 and discussed in depth in Chapter 8, close collaboration and consultation with a child psychiatrist who has expertise in treating moderate-to-severe pediatric OCD will ensure that patients receive evidence-based pharmacotherapy.
2. *Staffing.* There are pros and cons to running an intensive treatment program as a sole provider versus as a group of providers/staff members. A variety of staffing models are discussed in Chapter 6. Most current established intensive treatment programs for pediatric OCD include at least one psychologist and one or more additional staff members at the PhD/PsyD, master's-, or bachelor's level who work together as a team to help patients and families complete in-session exposures. One benefit of this team-based approach is that the patient can practice and generalize skills across multiple treatment providers. Another benefit is that a greater number of providers may result in faster identification of various OCD symptoms that may not have been reported during the initial assessment. Similarly, more providers means that more therapists can contribute to discussions around treatment planning and treatment process considerations that a single therapist working alone might miss

(e.g., ideas for exposures, how to triage symptoms, how to work on symptoms conjointly). Simultaneously, more than one therapist on a team necessitates that providers communicate well with one another, potentially on a daily basis, in order to ensure that treatment continues smoothly and successfully for the patient. Larger teams or those who do not overlap and check in at the start of each treatment day/session may find this challenging and may need to create and monitor a documentation system related to patient progress at each session. Just as communication with the patient and family is critical, consistent and clear communication between treatment team members will ensure that the treatment is effective and efficient.

While a therapist who does not collaborate with other providers on a team does not need to communicate and monitor communication systems in a patient's intensive treatment, sole providers may find intensive treatment stressful and/or experience burnout. Working with a single child or adolescent for 3 to 15 or more hours per week can be both extremely rewarding and extremely difficult in cases where there are challenges. Some, but not all, of the challenges that may increase provider stress include a child or caregiver who has low motivation for treatment, a family that does not follow through with between-session practice, and a patient who experiences very severe symptoms that may take several weeks to start improving. Moreover, if there are difficulties with therapist–patient "fit" more broadly, the family and sole therapist alike may experience frustration, which may in turn interfere with the therapist's effectiveness at work and/or the child and family's willingness and ability to participate and obtain benefit. We discuss these issues further in Chapter 5.

3. *Therapist training.* As discussed in Chapter 1, therapists preparing to start an intensive treatment program or option in their practices should already have training in the outpatient treatment of pediatric OCD and have at least some experience with treating moderate-to-severe symptoms in youth. If therapists are not experts in this domain, we strongly urge them to obtain access to colleagues who are experts and are willing to consult on cases. Similarly, in intensive treatment settings where bachelor's level, master's level, or other staff members without specialized training in pediatric OCD are either trainees or hired as staff, those individuals will need ongoing training, supervision, and/or consultation.

4. *Consultation for symptom-specific treatment.* Even the most expert OCD treatment therapists may need to obtain outside consultation for individual patients' symptoms. In our collective experience, we regularly consult with a wide variety of providers who have expertise in other forms of psychopathology for which we must often conduct differential diagnosis from OCD. While the following list is not exhaustive, we include a few of the more common types of providers with whom we

regularly consult during treatment of severe pediatric OCD. Access to colleagues with expertise in pediatric schizophrenia as well as with neurodevelopmental (including autism spectrum) disorders will allow for consultation on the not-rare occasions when such differential diagnostic issues occur. Patients with comorbid eating disorder symptoms may require a nutritionist to provide a meal plan and conduct regular follow-ups with patients and caregivers. Some patients who have contamination symptoms also present with histories of functional somatic complaints, allergies, or other medical concerns that require medical chart review and/or consultation with medical experts in those domains (often, but not always, the individual patient's medical providers). Given the common presentation of scrupulosity symptoms and religious obsessions in patients, access to religious figureheads for consultation may also be a crucial component of treatment. The therapist should consider how, when, and where to obtain such consultation and develop relationships with potential consultants in advance of offering intensive treatment so that there is no delay in identifying relevant consultants when the need for consultation arises.

5. *Physical space in and adjacent to the treatment setting.* There are some important considerations for physical space that may make the intensive treatment setting more comfortable and productive for participating patients and families. These are discussed in detail in Chapters 4 and 5. However, we mention space herein, as it is a critical aspect of treatment for the therapist to consider prior to starting an intensive program.

WHO IS THE IDEAL TARGET YOUTH FOR INTENSIVE OCD TREATMENT?

As indicated in Chapter 2, intensive treatment can be effective across a number of settings and with a wide range of children and adolescents. We have found many types of patients and families to be good candidates for intensive treatment. We first discuss the characteristics of patients with moderate OCD symptoms who may be good candidates, then turn to patients with more severe symptoms, and finally discuss considerations for patients with diagnostic comorbidity for whom intensive treatment may be particularly helpful.

Patients with moderate OCD symptoms who are initial (i.e., once-weekly outpatient) cognitive behavioral therapy (CBT) nonresponders may benefit from the increase in treatment intensity and symptom management. The parents of such patients may also be more motivated to comply with between-session practice if this was an issue in weekly outpatient treatment. Similarly, patients in the moderate symptom range who are highly motivated for treatment and/or would like to engage in treatment during an opportune time (e.g., summer break) may respond much more quickly in intensive, as compared to once-weekly outpatient, treatment. In such instances, we encourage intensive treatment if the family can devote the time, effort, and resources (including financial). Patients in the moderate symptom range may also be good candidates for intensive treatment if a parent engages in significant enough accommodation that it begins to interfere with family functioning. In these cases, once-weekly outpatient treatment may be insufficient with regard to time needed in order to do in-session ERP and simultaneously work with the family to reduce blame, conflict, and/or accommodation.

Patients with OCD symptoms in the moderate-to-severe range are ideal candidates for intensive treatment, as their symptoms typically cause significant functional impairments and distress for the youth and/or family. For example, a patient who is no longer able to attend school, participate in extracurricular activities, or complete activities of daily living may need an intensive approach to regain prior levels of functioning and return to expected developmentally appropriate roles. Intensive treatment may be particularly appropriate for patients who are not able to attend school or complete assignments; participation in intensive treatment would not remove them from academic demands if their OCD already prevents them from engaging in school. Importantly, if a patient *is* able to successfully participate in academics despite moderate-to-severe symptoms, intensive treatment during school hours may not be appropriate since in most circumstances intensive treatment *would* interfere with academics. In considering whether intensive treatment is appropriate for a patient in the mild-to-moderate range, the therapist may consider the cost/benefit ratio of potentially removing the patient from activities in which they are able to participate meaningfully or consider programs that are minimally disruptive to these activities.

When patients have plans for discharge from inpatient or residential treatment, an intensive setting may provide more support than once-weekly outpatient treatment during the patient's return home and to daily life. In these situations, we strongly recommend intensive treatment or a partial hospital program as the step-down from inpatient or residential treatment. In addition to providing better support of the patient and family during the transition back home, it may reduce the likelihood of needing readmission to inpatient or residential care. This graded step from inpatient or residential to intensive treatment may allow for the patient to continue making gains related to symptom reduction and prepare for another subsequent step-down to outpatient care.

Finally, a note about diagnostic comorbidity. As indicated in Chapter 1, comorbidity in pediatric OCD is the norm rather than the exception. For some patients, OCD treatment can be clearly prioritized without any safety or treatment issues. For example, a child may have primary OCD in the moderate-to-severe range and co-occurring separation anxiety disorder. If the initial evaluation reveals that the OCD is more distressing and impairing, both the family and clinician may agree that OCD treatment is the priority. Similarly, a patient may have OCD in the moderate-to-severe range and also have mild-to-moderate neurodevelopmental disorder symptoms, such as of autism spectrum disorder (ASD). If there are no immediate treatment concerns for ASD and the patient is able to communicate symptoms enough to participate in OCD treatment, prioritizing OCD may make sense. In other circumstances, the symptoms of the comorbid diagnosis may be significant enough that they would interfere with treatment of the OCD. For example, a patient with ASD who engages in aggressive behavior whenever distressed or exhibits extremely rigid and inflexible thinking, with an inability to participate in exposures, may require a more comprehensive treatment program that can address the aggression or inflexibility either in tandem or before addressing OCD. Similarly, a patient may have uncontrolled attention-deficit/hyperactivity disorder (ADHD) symptoms with significant inattention, hyperactivity, or impulsivity that interferes with the ability to comply with therapist requests, causing the entire session to be spent redirecting the patient to focus on OCD; such patients may require a different type or level of care or effective pharmacotherapy for their ADHD prior to enrolling in the intensive OCD treatment. We continue this discussion regarding comorbidity in Chapter 7 in the discussion of candidates for whom intensive specialized OCD treatment may not be appropriate.

WHAT KINDS OF PATIENTS MAY NOT BE GOOD CANDIDATES FOR INTENSIVE OCD TREATMENT?

Some patients may require a higher level of care or a different treatment approach than specialized intensive treatment for pediatric OCD. We first discuss symptom and diagnostic concerns and then discuss some considerations related to family ability and motivation to participate.

First, patients with OCD symptoms in the mild-to-moderate range who have never previously attempted a course of outpatient ERP could benefit from an "expedited dose" via intensive treatment, although these patients might also sufficiently benefit from once-weekly outpatient treatment. Important considerations for such patients and families include whether the patient and caregivers are willing and able to participate in intensive treatment (i.e., in regard to finances, time, childcare for other children, etc.), as well as whether intensive treatment would interfere with domains of functioning in which the patient is able to participate (e.g., school, extracurricular activities). We generally recommend that outpatient treatment be attempted first if symptoms are in the mild-to-moderate range and intensive treatment would disrupt the patient's current functioning (e.g., they are generally doing well in school and socially) and/or disrupt the parent's employment or other demands.

In contrast, OCD may be so severe that a higher level of specialized treatment is warranted. For example, some OCD symptoms may be so severe that the youth cannot leave their room or home and need to be hospitalized in an inpatient or residential facility in order to access treatment. Similarly, if family dynamics and/or parental stress or psychopathology has resulted in an environment that would make intensive treatment (where the patient is still living at home) difficult, a higher level of care in which the patient is removed from the home (i.e., residential) may provide a context in which the patient can benefit from treatment while other family members simultaneously pursue intervention for their difficulties.

Some comorbidities may require more immediate treatment prior to addressing OCD. For example, active suicidality or nonsuicidal self-injury, depressive symptoms that are so significant that the patient is not able to complete in- and between-session practice, and/or bipolar disorder, schizophrenia, or eating disorders that are uncontrolled and require immediate treatment should all be addressed prior to treating OCD. Finally, there may be symptoms of some disorders that interfere with treatment compliance. For example, disruptive behavior such as defiance or aggression may interfere with in-session and at-home practice and require more immediate treatment. Comorbid depression with significant negative thinking that leads to guilt and hopelessness, negative affect that leads to amotivation and disinterest in doing anything (including treatment), and/or vegetative symptoms that make it extremely difficult for the patient to even get out of bed or off the couch, even in the absence of suicidality, may require more immediate treatment. Again, in these cases we recommend sequencing treatment so that the treatment-interfering symptoms are addressed first and OCD addressed subsequently. We discuss how to consider and screen for these diagnoses and interfering symptoms via the assessment process in Chapter 7.

In some families, the patient or parent may refuse treatment or otherwise display lack of motivation to work on OCD symptoms. If the difficulty is with the patient, motivational interviewing and/or rewards may be helpful in bringing the patient to a point of agreeing to participate. At other times, the patient may continue to refuse treatment and the family might be referred for parent training, family therapy, or some other modality in which the parent might obtain benefit while the patient has time to reconsider willingness to participate. If the difficulty is with one parent in a two-parent household, but the other parent is willing to participate, the therapist might proceed with further assessment of whether and how the reticent parent's stance may or may not interfere with the child's treatment. Given that most patients live with and are at least somewhat dependent on a caregiver, and given that OCD is a disorder that tends to affect the whole family unit, we do not recommend treating children and adolescents without at least some caregiver involvement. However, some older adolescents may be able to successfully participate in treatment primarily on their own. In such cases, we encourage therapists to be aware of their state laws regarding consent and treatment and to consider the implications of treating the adolescent without involving a parent or caregiver.

DISCUSSING EXPECTATIONS WITH FAMILIES BEFORE EMBARKING ON INTENSIVE TREATMENT

Regardless of the specific intensive treatment model, there are several things that the patients and family should know *before* they make a commitment to intensive treatment. This way, there will be no surprises for the patient and/or family, and they will be prepared for treatment intensity. Although not exhaustive, below we provide a list of some considerations that might be discussed during a clinician's recommendation that the family pursue intensive treatment of OCD.

1. *Dates and times of treatment participation*, as well as expectation for between-session practice. Some considerations for the family may include childcare for other children, parent taking time off of work or patient taking time off from school or extracurriculars, and cost.

2. *Length of treatment.* Some programs require that the family make a commitment of a specific number of weeks/months as a starting point in order to ensure that they are able to engage in a sufficient treatment dose. For example, it is rare that 1 week of treatment consisting of 10 treatment hours total will be sufficient for a patient in the moderate-to-severe symptom range. Treatment length may or may not be standardized across all patients and may also be reduced or lengthened as the patient proceeds through treatment. If treatment will overlap with holidays, school breaks, or family vacations, you may also provide expectations or have discussions with the family about what this might mean for treatment and/or whether waiting until after the break is warranted.

3. *Parental involvement.* A clear and explicit conversation about parental involvement will also be important and may depend, in part, on patient age, type of symptoms, parental accommodation or involvement in compulsions, and so forth. Discussions regarding parental involvement should always include factors such as how many treatment hours per week parents are expected to participate, whether they can bring their work with them if they will have some downtime, and parental monitoring of symptoms. Depending on the family context and involvement with symptoms, other family members may be asked to come to one or more sessions and participate in between-session practice. It will also be helpful to discuss, in the case of homes where the patient has two or more caregivers, who will come to treatment: one parent who will then be expected to convey information to other caregivers for consistency or two or more caregivers who will take turns and keep each other informed after sessions. This is especially true when youth live in more than one household with separate caregiver(s) in each. In some families, siblings also play a role in either accommodation or compulsions (or say or do things that are unhelpful to the affected patient) and may need to participate or receive guidance from the therapist or parents.

4. *Expectations for exposures and other skills learned.* An explicit conversation with both the patient and parents should include that both patient and parent are expected to participate in sessions, as well as in completion of between-session practice assignments. We have found it helpful to balance between firmness about treatment compliance and

clarify that typically at-home practice often won't take more than 10 to 30 additional minutes per day and will ultimately result in less time spent on compulsions, but that this between-session practice is necessary in order for treatment to be successful.

5. *Considerations for group intervention.* If any part of the intensive treatment involves group work, the family should be made aware of this before starting. In such cases, the confidentiality threshold may be lower than in individual outpatient treatment, and ongoing discussions and reminders about trying to maintain confidentiality within the group may help patients and parents feel comfortable to participate openly. Relatedly, patients may feel nervous or concerned about group work due to embarrassment about specific OCD symptoms (e.g., fears of contamination or harm avoidance), social anxiety, or general hesitations about participating in treatment. Transparent, open conversations about what will versus will not be shared in group may help to allay fears. In some cases, group involvement may be incorporated in a stepwise way into ERP as with an exposure hierarchy.

6. *Motivational interviewing as a tool for treatment engagement.* Even when a patient and family are willing to participate in treatment, motivational interviewing can be a powerful tool. Linking how intensive treatment for OCD will help the patient reach their personal goals or improve aspects of their lives that *the patient or family wants to improve* may be especially salient, rather than simply focusing on the idea that the OCD symptoms themselves should reduce. For example, some patients may feel that their symptoms are protective or that they don't need treatment, but may be motivated by the idea that once symptoms sufficiently reduce, they would be able to do something with friends that they are currently unable to do because OCD interferes. Other patients may be motivated by a return to school or extracurricular activities. Still others may be primarily motivated by future events that they feel they could not currently achieve based on symptoms, such as an ability to have sleepovers or go to college one day. Using the family's goals for the patient more broadly may help to increase willingness and motivation to comply with treatment.

In summary, there are many practical benefits of intensive treatment for pediatric OCD. At the same time, there are several important considerations for therapists, some of which should be considered in concert with each individual family, prior to deciding whether intensive treatment is appropriate and the most likely approach to alleviate the patient's symptoms. Together, this information suggests that clinicians should be thoughtful and deliberate as they develop their intensive treatment framework, secure space, and work with OCD-affected patients and their families. Such intentional decisions will increase the likelihood that intensive treatment and the setting in which it is provided will be maximally effective for the patient and family to learn how to manage and reduce symptoms.

CHAPTER 3 TAKE-HOME POINTS

- An increased number of intervention hours in a given week can allow for faster traction on symptom reduction.
- The potential for greater gains and symptom reduction in a shorter period of time may also decrease functional impairment more quickly, which allows patients to return to age-appropriate and expected activities.
- Some patients may be able to complete the majority of treatment over a winter/summer break and resume school on the same timeline as their peers.
- Patients with OCD symptoms in the moderate-to-severe range are ideal candidates for intensive treatment, as their symptoms typically cause significant functional impairments and distress for the child and family.
- While there are many practical benefits of intensive treatment for pediatric OCD, therapists and family should be thoughtful about important considerations to determine whether intensive treatment is an appropriate fit.

Program Format: Balancing Structure and Flexibility

Chapter 3 provided details about the clinical benefits of and broad considerations for running intensive treatments for pediatric obsessive compulsive disorder (OCD). In this chapter, we describe the specific considerations related to an intensive treatment program's structure. These include daily program hours, total number of hours per week, relative number of group versus individual sessions, and how to provide flexibility and options for individual participants within a larger program framework. The chapter closes with a review of optimal facilities and physical space in various settings, as well as ideal institutional support for maintaining an intensive program in the long term.

HOW INTENSIVE IS INTENSIVE? CORE TREATMENT COMPONENT AND HOURS

As described in Chapters 2 and 3, intensive treatment can be successful in a variety of settings and with a variety of formats. This includes variability in the number and scheduling of program hours and treatment days and length of treatment in weeks. For example, in some programs, intensive treatment consists of a 3-hour session, 3 days per week, while in others it can be 3 or more hours per day for 4 or 5 days per week. The most important aspect of increasing intensity is the intensification of the core treatment ingredient: exposure and response prevention (ERP). Exposures (many, many of them) must be done in each treatment session. In our experience, active engagement in exposures constitutes at least 70% of each treatment session in an intensive setting. For example, in contrast to a once-weekly outpatient ERP treatment in which 30 to 40 minutes may be spent on exposures in one 45-minute session, many children and adolescents can engage in up to 2 hours and 30 minutes of exposures at a time, some even without a break, as part of a 3-hour treatment day, for 4 days per week for an extended duration (e.g., 8–12 weeks). Some of our colleagues have also published data (see Table A.2 in the Appendix) that patients can participate in up to 8 hours of intensive treatment in a single day, with the vast majority of this time in exposure, broken up by lunch and other brief breaks. Thus, it is *primarily the intensity of exposures* that constitutes intensive treatment.

There are a variety of ways to arrange program hours and days per week to intensify ERP. Irrespective of the number of hours, days, and weeks, intensive treatment programs fill a specific gap between once- or twice-weekly outpatient therapy and more acute (e.g., psychiatric partial hospitalization, residential, or inpatient hospitalization) programs. While some insurers consider intensive treatment programs as still within the "outpatient" (as compared to inpatient/hospitalization) realm, others are considered part of partial hospitalization programs. Both such cases are consistent with an intensive treatment model's goal of the patient living at home and attending portions of life activities (whether academic, extracurricular, and/or social) that have not been negatively impacted by OCD. In contrast, acute care settings pull patients out of other settings (home, school) to participate in treatment. Intensive treatment aims to strike a balance between significantly increasing the intensity of treatment as compared to traditional outpatient treatment, without removing patients from activities in which they are not functionally impaired. One way to consider how to intensify treatment is based on how intensive programs "fit" between twice-weekly hourly outpatient sessions and partial hospitalization programs (which typically operate 6 to 8 hours, 5 days per week). In our collective experience, we tend to define intensive treatment as comprising a minimum of 3 hours per week, with sessions spread across multiple treatment days, and ranging up to 15+ hours per week. We view this 3-hour minimum as sufficient to maximize time spent in exposures, while also leaving sufficient time to learn augmentation treatment strategies (e.g., mindfulness, distress tolerance skills) and address other relevant issues (e.g., parental accommodation, comorbidity) without reducing ERP time. However, as discussed above, there are a variety of ways to increase session time per week. For example, some pediatric OCD intensive programs condense weekly treatment time into a single 8-hour day once or twice (or more times) per week. The maximum number of hours that constitutes intensive treatment may also be dictated by systemic (e.g., hospital or insurer) rules about how intensive treatment can be billed. Regardless of the specific maximum hours per day, week, or total number of weeks, conceptually and practically intensive OCD programs differ from time and activities in other acute care programs. We have included a few sample intensive treatment schedules below to illustrate how time in treatment might be allocated. In this schedule, ERP is conducted in both individual and group formats, although group work also includes mindfulness and other cognitive behavioral therapy (CBT) exercises. A detailed sample group is provided further in this chapter.

Sample schedule for 1 week of a program that does not have a set maximum number of weeks

Monday	Tuesday	Wednesday	Thursday
		3:15–4 p.m. INDIVIDUAL	3:15–4 p.m. FAMILY
4–6 p.m. GROUP	4–6 p.m. GROUP		4–6 p.m. GROUP
6–6:45 p.m. INDIVIDUAL			

Sample schedule of a program that operates over a 3-week period:

	Monday	Tuesday	Wednesday	Thursday	Friday
Week 1	90-minute session: Psychoeducation	90-minute session: ERP	90-minute session: ERP	90-minute session: Other CBT skills	90-minute session: ERP
Week 2	90-minute session: ERP	90-minute session: ERP	90-minute session: Other CBT skills	90-minute session: ERP	90-minute session: ERP
Week 3	90-minute session: ERP	90-minute session: ERP		90-minute session: Maintenance and relapse prevention	90-minute session: Maintenance and relapse prevention

Sample 1-week intensive (e.g., during a school break)

	Monday	Tuesday	Wednesday	Thursday	Friday
10–11 a.m.	Homework Review Psychoeducation and other CBT skills				
11–12:30	Exposure practices				
	Break				
1:30–3 p.m.	Exposure practices				
3–3:30	Daily Review Assignment of homework practices				

As mentioned above, there is a wide range of options regarding the structure and appropriate number of treatment hours in an intensive program, and many factors may be considered when deciding a program's schedule. We encourage providers to schedule their intensive treatment hours after school if possible so that patients enrolled do not fall further behind in their academics. In some instances, regardless of the intensive program hours or length of admission, the therapist may want to pre-emptively consider how to work with parents and schools if the patient is to miss school and determine what the academic expectations might be during intensive treatment. Other setup considerations related to the family may include whether a patient is able to tolerate distress if treatment takes place over several hours per day or whether breaks or other activities would need to be scheduled in between ERP practices. Similarly, the number of hours and sessions per week may influence whether a parent is able to participate (e.g., leave work early) or would be required to take a family medical leave (e.g., if treatment were upward of 20 hours per week). In our experience, it is helpful to maintain some flexibility, such that the therapist communicates with parents prior to admission about academic expectations and time commitments, and then the therapist and family can work together with the patient's school based on symptoms and severity, anticipated length of stay, and so forth.

Finally, there are other decisions that may be helpful to consider prior to opening an intensive program. For example, will the program setup in regard to hours/days/weeks be identical for all patients, or might there be flexibility based on need, or even exceptions for some families? If the program has a minimum number of treatment weeks, but a family is traveling far to receive treatment and will be living in a hotel during treatment, would a shorter length of treatment time be considered? Similarly, will the program accommodate a patient who previously completed intensive treatment in that program, and a year later needs some booster sessions that likely will not result in a second full course of treatment because the patient has not experienced a full relapse? It is important for the therapist to consider such characteristics of the program that may influence a family's ability and willingness to participate up front, and balance such flexibility with some consistency based on the evidence base for how much intensive treatment time is likely necessary for the average patient with moderate-to-severe OCD to maximally benefit from treatment.

Therapist and program considerations may also intersect with total treatment time per week. For example, if more than one therapist works in the intensive program, consider how staff will communicate and maintain consistency across sessions for individual patients and across patients and families. Similarly, consider if staffing with two or more treatment providers might allow a program to offer more treatment hours. This intersects with the anticipated number of patients that the program can effectively accommodate at any given time. The combination of therapists and patients (and parents) impact space needs (discussed further below and in Chapter 5), or conversely, space constraints may impact the possible number of therapists and/or families that a program can accommodate. Each of these considerations may influence the initial setup of the intensive treatment in regard to whether the program occurs for fewer longer days (e.g., two 6-hour days per week) or more frequent yet relatively shorter (e.g., 3 hours several times per week) sessions. For additional discussion of staffing considerations related to a sole provider versus two or more providers on a team, see Chapters 3 and 6.

WEEKLY STRUCTURE OF AN INTENSIVE TREATMENT PROGRAM

Just as maintaining an agenda and structure in an hour-long outpatient therapy appointment is important, structure is arguably even more important in intensive treatment of pediatric OCD. First, the intensity of treatment, which is often associated with OCD severity, indicates that there is no time to waste. Families may feel desperate, or express concern that the intensive treatment program is their last opportunity to help their children experience relief from symptoms before an admission to residential, partial hospitalization, or inpatient setting. Second, a clear and transparent structure will help manage expectations on the part of a patient and family about the intensity of treatment itself, including how much time will be spent in exposures, and that specific other activities (e.g., mindfulness, distress tolerance, group work, scheduled breaks) are deliberately included rather than added randomly and without consideration. These other activities can also serve as natural, yet expected and planned, breaks between exposures. Third, some of the most successful patients in our respective intensive programs have been those who clearly understood and planned to arrive to treatment ready to work just as they would be prepared to exercise when they arrived to the gym or an extracurricular sport activity. Rather than spending time negotiating whether and how much time to spend on exposures (as may occur in outpatient treatment), a consistent and clear schedule in intensive treatment can prepare patients for long and focused treatment sessions in which exposures are the core ingredient.

We view several treatment components as necessary parts of the weekly treatment schedule. First, each treatment session should start with a review of homework, or between-session practice, that the patient was previously assigned in the last session. This review may also occur in concert with a check-in with the parent regarding parental monitoring, and worsening or improvements in symptoms they have noticed since the last session. This "review since last session" can provide a context within which to link the exposures from the prior intensive session to the current one and help the clinician consider whether planned exposures for this session need to be modified based on the patient's successful completion of, or distress during, between-session practice.

As discussed previously and as discussed in Chapter 11, ERP is the core effective ingredient in treatment. Thus, each intensive session should primarily consist of conducting, and not merely planning, exposure exercises with the patient. We also recommend that treatment sessions include other skills (see Chapters 12, 13, and 14 for specifics), although not every skill may be necessary in every session or appropriate for every patient.

One set of skills that we believe provides helpful augmentation of exposures is mindfulness (see Chapter 13). A brief experiential mindfulness practice and subsequent discussion of how mindfulness skills can be used to respond to obsessions provides a brief break between exposures and also provides patients with practice in a skill that they might apply during their management of OCD in their daily lives.

Parent and/or family interventions might also occur daily, depending on the patient age and parent involvement in symptoms (e.g., accommodation). If the parent is not involved in symptoms and there are not natural exposures for which involving the parent would titrate exposure difficulty, parent/family intervention meetings throughout the week may still be useful (in addition to the parent check-in during homework review at the start of session). The content of such meetings might include how parents can set limits for co-occurring behavioral problems and/or in responding to OCD in a way that is consistent with the patient's current stage of treatment, providing support and validation for parenting frustrations and/or ongoing psychoeducation to manage treatment expectations, and so forth.

We also recommend a regular psychiatrist check-in as part of intensive treatment for purposes of medication management and maintenance (see Chapter 8).

Finally, the session should end with a review of activities covered that day and clear and specific plans for at-home practice before the next session (including youth and parent agreement to the assigned practices). We provide an example of how some of these elements and structure may be incorporated into a group session, with multiple patients focused on a wide range of symptoms:

SAMPLE GROUP					
4–4:15 p.m.: Exposure homework review with REWARD					
4:15–5 p.m.: Skill! Cognitive restructuring					
5–5:50 p.m.: Exposure practice					
Patient 1: Reaching out to friends from school	Patient 2: Touching bathroom items without washing	Patient 3: Saying no to peers' requests	Patient 4: Watching a movie that has triggered OCD thoughts	Patient 5: Typing without deleting/retyping	Patient 6: Interoceptive exposures and eating in front of peers
5:50–6 p.m.: Exposure review with REWARD; homework planning					

Another final component that occurs at the very end of treatment is a graduation or celebratory activity in which the therapist, parent, and patient can all acknowledge the patient's successes and accomplishments. In treatment settings that involve at least some group work, involving other patients and parents currently enrolled in an intensive treatment program can provide an additional layer of praise for the patient who is graduating and provide hope and motivation for those newer to the program. Separate from relapse prevention (discussed in Chapter 14), we view a celebration at the end of treatment as one additional means of encouraging the patient and family to maintain motivation and continue using the skills they have learned as they transition to outpatient care.

GROUP VERSUS INDIVIDUAL INTENSIVE TREATMENT

There are certainly benefits to group treatment and to individual treatment. In regard to individual treatment, only one therapist is required, patients can participate based on their and the therapist's schedules, and each patient can work at their own rate without consideration of other patients. However, there are some distinct advantages of treatment that includes a group component (regardless of the amount of time spent in group). As described in Chapter 3, group treatment provides a context to normalize the experience of OCD and the difficulty of exposure-based treatment. Group intervention can also allow patients with similar symptoms to work on exposures together. We have found that this social motivation increases engagement in and compliance with in- and between-session practice. Additionally, although programs that include a group component typically require more than one therapist, the presence of two or more therapists can allow for one to lead a group for patients, while the other checks in with or runs a group for parents. It can also facilitate pulling individual patients out of the group, one at a time, for family work or individual discussions that are more challenging in the group context.

If treatment does include a group component, it might be useful to split the individual and group time in a standardized way. For example, individual intervention might be focused on exposures for specific symptoms, particularly those that might be embarrassing or inappropriate (e.g., due to other patients' ages) to discuss in group, better discussed when parents are present, and so forth. Individual intervention might also focus on parent involvement in exposures. In contrast, group intervention might be focused on activities that are less specific to an individual patient's symptoms and more focused on skills that would be beneficial for all patients (e.g., mindfulness, distress tolerance, a planned break). The patient and therapist might also agree during individual treatment time that the patient will participate in a specific set of exposures in the group, assuming that the patient can do so safely and willingly in front of others. For some patients with similar symptoms, group work with one or two other patients who can serve as exposure targets for one another may be particularly useful. As discussed in Chapter 3, other variables such as staffing and patient ages/developmental levels are also factors to consider when deciding on group activities, and these may change over time depending on the specific milieu of the group.

FLEXIBILITY WITHIN FIDELITY: PROVIDING FAMILIES WITH EVIDENCE-BASED OPTIONS IN INTENSIVE TREATMENT

Depending on the setup of the intensive treatment program, there may be opportunities to provide families with evidence-based options even in the context of a structured program. For some patients, it may make more sense to allow a shorter time in treatment (e.g., patient has OCD symptoms in the mild range and will participate for 3 weeks during winter break) or fewer days/shorter sessions per week (e.g., patient previously completed intensive treatment successfully, but recurrence of symptoms without a full relapse suggests that additional intensive treatment may be helpful). Co-occurring interventions that do not target the patient's OCD (e.g., family therapy, parent OCD treatment, nutrition consultation for co-occurring eating disorder symptoms) may also be warranted and outside the scope of specialty pediatric OCD intensive treatment. Planning in advance for a patient to reduce the number of hours in intensive treatment as part of a taper prior to discharge can help to both generalize skills learned in treatment as they reintegrate into daily activities and identify final symptom areas to address before discharge.

If intensive treatment includes a group component, there may also be some room for flexibility for individual patients even while maintaining structure within treatment across youth. For example, if a patient's symptoms would otherwise prohibit them from participating completely in group at the start of treatment (e.g., social anxiety concerns about being in a group context), slow integration of the patient into the group as part of a set of exposures could be especially helpful. Similarly, for some patients, group work may be particularly helpful, as it allows for exposure practice with peers (e.g., patient agreeing with the therapist to ask another patient to touch and "contaminate" something that belongs to them).

Flexibility for caregivers that will participate in treatment with the patient may also be ideal or even necessary in some circumstances. For example, some co-parents may request that they take turns participating in treatment, or that one parent attend treatment exclusively. In other households, parents may ask that an additional caregiver (e.g., grandparent) who lives in the home and is involved in the patient's upbringing participate because both parents must work. The most important considerations here are that core information about treatment, including what is expected from the patient and family members, is conveyed to all relevant parties. That said, it may be useful in families with more than one parent or caregiver for all caregivers to participate in some components of treatment (e.g., an early treatment session for purposes of psychoeducation; a later treatment session if it becomes clear that caregivers are not consistently responding to obsessions without accommodation).

A variety of other opportunities for flexibility in program setup and treatment may be relevant. We encourage any providers who may consider developing an intensive treatment to spend some time thinking through these in advance, as they may influence physical infrastructure such as space and technology, staffing decisions, and how the program is presented to patients and families.

INCLUSION OF PATIENTS WITH PRIMARY NON-OCD ANXIETY DISORDERS

There may be some circumstances in which patients with non-OCD anxiety disorders at moderate-to-severe levels might also benefit from attending an intensive treatment program that is largely geared toward OCD. If treatment is individual and does not include any group components, this would be a non-issue, and intensive treatment could be appropriate. However, there are some considerations if the OCD intensive treatment does include a group component. Specifically, while older patients may be able to differentiate between their peers' description of symptoms, including compulsions from their own fears/worries where compulsions are not present, some younger patients may become confused about how the OCD cycle (and group discussions around ERP) may be consistent versus inconsistent with their own anxiety symptoms and exposure-based treatment. Additionally, if the group contains more than two patients and the majority of patients have OCD as their treatment target, a single patient whose treatment target is non-OCD anxiety may feel isolated or "different." Nonetheless, there have been circumstances in our own intensive treatment programs where a patient with non-OCD anxiety was included in a group of other patients with OCD, and the above considerations have not been concerns for either the patient or parents. The therapist developing an intensive treatment program may decide on some broad parameters about inclusion of non-OCD anxiety in a group-based program, with some flexibility depending on the specific group milieu at any given time and individual patient's anxiety symptoms. Throughout, however, the therapist should provide clear communication to the patient with non-OCD anxiety (and their parent) about which aspects of group intervention do versus do not apply and how to consider the substitutions that are needed (e.g., the OCD cycle during psychoeducation would look slightly different from an anxiety cycle, with "avoidance" instead of "compulsions" as a way to alleviate distress).

ROLLING VERSUS COHORT ADMISSIONS (FOR PROGRAMS THAT INVOLVE A GROUP COMPONENT)

Depending on the intensive treatment program's setup, rolling admissions may occur, such that for each discharged patient, a new one is admitted. Some of the benefits of this approach in the group setting is that patients and families who are further along in the program can serve as models for or provide information to those who are newer to the program; additionally, it allows for easier scheduling of admissions by eliminating the need to wait for a set cohort start date. Depending on the amount of time spent in group interventions, this also means that some patients may be working on very high-level and difficult exposures, while others are doing much smaller exposures for briefer periods of time, comparatively. Another approach to admissions is to have a set length of treatment (e.g., 12 weeks), with cohorts of patients admitted at the same time. Some benefits of this approach are that therapists can teach skills to all patients at once, and that there may be more consistency in skill implementation and expectations across patients. However, this cohort admissions approach requires that families be able and willing to start treatment at the same time, and that the program have a steady flow of prospective participants so that each new cohort is ready to begin as soon as the prior cohort completes treatment. The cohort approach may also be less flexible than rolling admissions in that it requires all patients to participate for the same length and intensity of treatment, potentially regardless of an individual patient's treatment needs.

TELEHEALTH

Increasingly, telehealth is becoming recognized as a valid and safe intervention modality. The American Psychological Association and a variety of other organizations now include free webinars and trainings for implementation of telehealth with children and adolescents. Telehealth may be particularly useful as a supplemental treatment modality in intensive treatment. For example, if one of an individual patient's OCD symptoms occurs exclusively in their home bathroom and no other bathrooms, video therapy using a secure service that is compliant with HIPAA (Health Insurance Privacy and Accountability Act of 1996) may allow for the therapist to virtually guide patients through exposures. Similarly, if a family has traveled a distance to participate in intensive treatment and their home is too far to return for booster/maintenance sessions, teletherapy may be an excellent modality. While a discussion of state/federal laws and ethics guidelines are outside the scope of this book, it is important for the clinician considering inclusion of telehealth into intensive treatment to be aware of state, licensing, and insurer laws/regulations, as well as ethical guidelines for virtual treatment.

There are also considerations specific to pediatric OCD that are critical for successful telehealth sessions. First, depending on the patient's symptoms, the therapist should consider how to determine if patients are actually engaging in response prevention, or whether they are completing compulsions, during telehealth sessions. Similarly, families should think about how they can set up video devices to ensure that the therapist is able to have a sense of the aspects of the space related to the patient's symptoms in order to devise appropriate exposures. Since the therapist is not physically present, make arrangements in advance in the event that the patient becomes distressed, upset, or the video connection is lost. On a more basic level, consider whether the patient is old and attentive enough to participate in telehealth independently or if a parent needs to be present for the entire session.

One additional consideration is that, as discussed in this chapter and elsewhere in this book, some of the most potent exposures in intensive treatment are those done outside of the therapy room in real-world settings (e.g., stores, restaurants, the patient's home environment, etc.). As with in-person exposures in public, telehealth sessions, particularly those in public, should take care to adhere to strict guidelines related to protect confidentiality for participants and ensuring that families are aware of risks associated with the conduct of treatment in public settings. When conducting exposure sessions in public spaces, we recommend the therapist remove any identification (e.g., their hospital ID badge) that would break confidentiality by making it obvious that the patient is engaging in mental health treatment. The therapist and patient should also have a conversation prior to leaving the office to determine the patient's preferred response should the patient see someone they know. Depending on the individuals living in the home environment, this may also be true in the patient's home.

PHYSICAL SPACE AND INFRASTRUCTURE

A variety of physical space considerations may make the intensive treatment setting more comfortable and productive for participating patients and families. We recommend considering how the physical space may meet the treatment program's needs for in-session treatment, including how many people maximum might be in the space at a given time; whether separate treatment rooms may be necessary for various treatment components that might occur simultaneously; and where parents will be when not in the treatment room with the child. For example, if a treatment program will have group-based treatment for patients to practice ERP exercises with one or more therapists *and* parents will simultaneously be in a parent group with another clinician, two rooms that fit all relevant individuals will be necessary. If there might be times when two patients are being treated individually by two separate providers and a third provider may be meeting with one or more parents, then at least three rooms may be necessary.

If the intensive treatment setting will include patients across a wide age range in the program at the same time, there may be a need for multiple therapy rooms so that the 5-year-old working on contamination symptoms does not observe the 17-year-old doing exposures to sexual and harm avoidance obsessions. We encourage providers to consider their space needs in the context of how their intensive program will operate, and we discuss this further in Chapter 5.

In addition, there are several critical elements to exposure-based treatment in an intensive setting that result in space and location needs outside of the therapy room. For example, contamination exposures often need to occur in bathrooms; physical proximity to a variety of bathrooms (e.g., bathroom in office building, as well as bathrooms in nearby restaurants and gas stations that may be more or less clean) will increase practice for generalization of gains across settings. A kitchen may be useful for exposures related to harm avoidance or food-related contamination. Access to stores, a library, classrooms, an emergency department or urgent care setting, religious buildings (e.g., church, synagogue, mosque), and other businesses will increase access to spaces in order to conduct creative exposures that emulate daily life activities and/or allow for overlearning (e.g., "If I can lay down on the public bus bench, I can certainly sleep on a bunk bed at camp that other kids have slept on"). Again, providers with less experience treating severe OCD will benefit from training and consultation in order to understand the tremendous range of types of exposure stimuli and settings necessary in order to sufficiently address the wide range of OCD symptom clusters.

Intensive treatment with more intervention hours per week involves greater intensity and number of exposures, and as described herein, aspects of the setting and its physical proximity to places and situations in which the patient's symptoms may be triggered will play an integral role.

CHAPTER 4 TAKE-HOME POINTS

- Program structures can vary greatly, and consideration of patient population, space, provider preferences, and team size is important.
- Regardless of the structure of any given program, the most important aspect of intensive treatment is the intensification of the core treatment ingredient: ERP. Exposures (many, many of them) must be done in each treatment session.
- Some of the most successful patients in our respective intensive programs have been those who clearly understood and planned to arrive to treatment ready to work. Planning, preparing families, and setting expectations are key to success.

Barriers, Challenges, and Solutions: Planning for Successful Program Implementation

Providers interested in implementing an intensive treatment model for obsessive compulsive disorder (OCD) should be aware of the potential challenges they may face during the process. Understanding and anticipating these in advance will maximize your opportunity to problem solve and develop a successful treatment program. Broadly speaking, there are three different types of barriers and challenges that clinicians should anticipate: (1) provider considerations, (2) consumer considerations, and (3) systems/infrastructure considerations. This chapter goes into more detail about each of these areas.

PROVIDER-SPECIFIC CONSIDERATIONS

As a therapist or group of providers, you must reflect on a number of personal and practice-specific factors when deciding to launch an intensive treatment program. In addition to the considerations outlined in Chapters 3 and 4, you should consider issues related to allocation of time, personal temperament and preferences, and staffing.

Intensive treatment requires an increased time commitment, not only on the part of patient, but also from the provider(s). A choice to develop intensive programming necessitates a reduction in the number of nonintensive individual patients you see in a given week to reserve space and time for intensive patients. You and your team must be comfortable with this trade-off and clearly understand what types of patients and models of treatment you prefer. Additionally, the nature of intensive programming and the possible addition of a group format may require more time in the week spent on strategic planning than typically done for individual patients. Implementing an intensive program in an already- busy practice will require shifting your patients with established therapy routines.

Alternatively, you might consider intensive programming as an expansion of services within your practice staffed by additional clinicians dedicated to intensive treatment. If an expansion of services, rather than a shift, is feasible, this will likely minimize disruption in clinical care for existing patients. Expansion and recruitment of additional clinicians will require a different time commitment related to oversight and supervision; when doing so, you should reflect ahead on your interest, comfort, and time available to serve in this supervisory manner, particularly if the model also relies on inclusion of trainees.

It will be helpful to consider the timing of an intensive program's hours within the day and the impact of this on flexibility for nonintensive patients. The frequency of intensive sessions often necessitates that they occur in "prime" after-school hours in order to allow pediatric patients to maintain normative school schedules. It is possible to conduct an intensive program during earlier daytime hours in order to preserve peak afternoon and evening hours for nonintensive patients. However, doing this can skew the intensive program toward the most severely impaired patients who are not able to attend school. This could increase the risk profile, reduce the range of patients within groups, increase duration of episodes of care, and decrease frequency of openings for new patients within your program. Lack of variability in patient severity may also shift group dynamics if the intensive program involves a group component, where positive peer pressure and encouragement related to peer success are important factors. Having sessions or groups primarily during school hours will additionally prevent you from working with patients directly on the transition back to school, which likely requires that your patient practice attending shorter, and then longer, parts of the schoolday. Keeping a patient out of school for longer than absolutely necessary may be detrimental and promote school avoidance.

Alternatively, you can preserve peak afternoon/evening hours for intensive programming by shifting use of other workday hours. Intake appointments and initial evaluations can be scheduled during structured times during the midday since these do not require an ongoing commitment for patients at a time that might be inconvenient. Additionally, attending to the issue of severity allows you to place the most severely impacted patients during midday hours. Flexible thinking will provide an array of alternative solutions. You may consider shifting the weekly schedule from the traditional Monday through Friday schedule to include either Saturday or Sunday as one of the intensive days. This can allow patients to attend one day a week when they do not have the obligations of school and can decompress the week for a therapist, who may then take a day off during the week instead. While these suggestions may seem obvious, in practice people often find it difficult to maintain these boundaries, which can lead to frustration and burnout. Being organized and disciplined once you select a model will help you be successful implementing these strategies over the long term.

Many of the decisions outlined above require that you and your team attend to your own temperament and personal preferences before considering an intensive program as part of your practice. Spend time reflecting on what type of clinical work you enjoy, what intensity of treatment and patient symptom severity you prefer, and your risk tolerance. Finally, some of these preferences and decisions may intersect with considerations discussed in Chapter 3, particularly physical space, setting, and whether you are already working as part of an embedded group practice or hospital team.

CONSUMER-SPECIFIC CONSIDERATIONS

Therapists developing intensive treatment programs also must attend to the potential barriers for patients of such programs. If these are not planned for and addressed, they may limit the success and sustainability of your program. The most common challenges faced by patients and their families relate to geography, cost, time commitment, and personal preferences.

Historically, one of the major challenges facing families has been finding a program in reasonable proximity to their home. Similarly, for therapists who want to develop an intensive treatment program, you must consider if your community can support such a program. In other words, is the local population base adequate to provide the program with referrals? With the recent rapid expansion of telehealth, including for intensive treatment, geography has become less of a barrier. This has its own potential challenges, as well as opportunities, and has yet to be studied extensively in the context of intensive treatment for OCD.

Cost is another common barrier for patients, particularly if the program utilizes an out-of-network, fee-for-service model. When planning an intensive program and deciding on the financial model, consider the local community and the needs of patients and providers within the institution(s) and the community. Centers, practices, and hospital systems whose models accept insurance still must attend to cost considerations given the emergence of high-deductible managed care plans, large co-insurance costs, and frequent limits to the number of reimbursed services in a given day. As a result, depending on how your program is billed, patients may still have high costs associated with an insurance-accepting program. Moreover, providers may be limited by the financial amount that insurance will reimburse for specific procedure codes in an outpatient model in order to make a program financially viable. An intensive program embedded within a formal partial hospitalization program or state-regulated intensive outpatient program (IOP) may require a specific number and type of sessions and may also regulate the length of stay for given patients. These requirements and reimbursement rates will vary between states and insurance providers; thus, the financial model and costs for patients and providers should be well planned.

Time commitment, for both the patients and caregivers, is frequently a barrier for families and needs to be accounted for in considering the timing and requirements of your program. With insurance-based models, there may be set requirements of number of service hours per week, but patients and families might be more willing to sign up for a full, required, program that is covered under an insurance plan than pay out of pocket. Conversely, an out-of-network model provides some additional choice and flexibility in terms of number of hours, timing, and required commitments; however, families may have more concerns about times that they are willing to participate. The timing of the program may interfere with work, school, homework, activities, and family obligations. Care should be taken in deciding the timing of the program to minimize this, and working with families to problem solve such barriers is critical to success. Equal care should be taken to plan the requirements of the program. For example, an overly rigid model requiring parental involvement at set times that interfere with work is unlikely to succeed.

Finally, patient preferences can be a barrier to recruitment. Some patients are reluctant to participate in groups, preferring individual therapy instead. This may relate to other underlying issues, such as social anxiety, feelings of embarrassment about their symptoms, or stigma about a diagnosis. Many of these barriers can be surmounted through careful psychoeducation during the initial contact and intake process. It is also helpful to engage in outreach and educate other providers in the community about the intensive model so that they understand it and can educate their patients effectively about it.

STRUCTURAL AND SYSTEMS CHALLENGES

Patient Population

One of the first tasks of planning an intensive treatment program is defining the target population. Different choices in this regard will lead to different potential challenges. You will need to define the ranges of ages and diagnoses that your program will serve, and some of this may be dependent on whether your program is part of a larger umbrella service, such as an outpatient service, partial hospitalization program, and/or embedded within a hospital or community healthcare setting.

The program can be designed to serve a specific age range or take a more inclusive approach with a broader range of participant ages. Each has its advantages and disadvantages. A narrower age range will allow for patients at the same developmental level to engage with one another, which may be more comfortable for patients and parents when considering a program. Conversely, having a very narrow age range may make it more difficult to fill program slots and maintain the census. Further, having patients of different ages and developmental levels within the same group can provide opportunities for positive peer encouragement and expectation, give older patients a sense of expertise and mastery, which they can then share with younger patients, and allow younger patients to "rise to the occasion." If you opt for a program that serves a large age range, you still might choose to cohort patients based on age, developmental stage, and specific symptom features. Any parent or patient concerns about the mixed groups typically can be addressed with psychoeducation during the intake process.

As referenced in previous chapters, the therapist must also decide on the range of diagnoses that will be included. Specifically, decide whether your program will only accept patients with OCD, or if you will accept patients with other disorders amenable to treatment with exposure-based cognitive behavioral therapy (CBT). Similar to the question of ages accepted to a program, a narrow range of qualifying diagnosis may make it more challenging to recruit and to maintain census in the program. On the flip side, qualifying criteria that are too broad may impact the effectiveness of the group experience, make planning interventions more challenging in the group setting, and make it more difficult to train and supervise trainees or other providers working under you who may not have expertise across the disorders related to OCD and anxiety. In addition to the question of alternative diagnoses related to OCD and anxiety, each provider developing an intensive program must define what other co-occurring disorders, which are not targets of the intensive treatment, are appropriate in the program (e.g., substance use disorders, externalizing disorders, major depressive disorder, personality disorders). We discuss this thoroughly in Chapter 7 in the description of the intake and assessment process. The inclusion of some co-occurring conditions may shift the group dynamics in an unhelpful way and may limit the effectiveness of the program. Depending on the specific symptoms and presentation, many of these patients may do better in your program after their comorbid condition is addressed elsewhere first. One of the main challenges for clinicians is maintaining fidelity to these boundaries and not letting them erode over time.

Finances, Regulatory Hurdles, and Managed Care

Once you define the patient population to be served, consider the financial model of the program. Many of these considerations will depend on the setting where you are implementing your model. Intensive treatments can be implemented as a specialized "track" in an inpatient setting or within a day program or partial hospital program (PHP), as a stand-alone intensive program, or as part of an existing outpatient practice.

If you are considering adding your programming to an inpatient or intermediate level of care (e.g., PHP), it is important to understand the billing structure of those programs, as they can vary greatly. Inpatient programs are generally bundle billed, meaning there is one daily charge for all clinical services delivered during that day, with no additional professional billing when you add a new group, individual session, or family session. In this case, you do not need to worry about reimbursement for these specific services. If the inpatient program does professional billing, it is critical to understand what you can bill for and how it will be reimbursed by insurance. These same considerations are important for an intermediate care setting like a day program or PHP, where you must understand the number and types of daily services required to qualify as a PHP. If you are integrating a new intensive program into an existing PHP, it is important to ensure that new services do not interfere with meeting the managed care requirements of a PHP. Many states require that an IOP is housed within an umbrella PHP or outpatient program, so we encourage you to explore your state-specific regulations and billing requirements. Working closely with clinical leadership and the finance team at the program is critical in these settings to prevent errors that would impact billing and provision of care.

If you are interested in starting a stand-alone intensive treatment program, keep in mind that an IOP is an official designation in many areas. As mentioned above, consider whether the IOP must be housed within a PHP or outpatient department or if it can serve as a stand-alone service. If you are operating within a fully established outpatient setting, you may opt not to use the official IOP designation and instead provide multiple outpatient sessions per week. How this works varies state to state, and your considerations may be based on whether your practice/clinic bills insurance or is out of network and fee for service. The simplest version, for the clinician, is the fee-for-service model. In this situation, one has the most freedom and flexibility to implement the program as desired, and you can simply bill each group, individual session, and family session separately to create the desired schedule. However, while this is the simplest and least financially risky approach for the clinician, it is important to keep in mind the impact on patients and their families. The fee-for-service approach limits who may enter the program and skews it toward a more affluent patient population or to those who have flexible and reliable out-of-network reimbursement benefits. It is important to think about the community you aim to serve and the patients you want to target for intensive treatment.

When working within a fee-for-service model, we recommend trying to minimize costs for families who wish to pursue out-of-network reimbursement by being thoughtful about types of sessions that can be reimbursed (e.g., instead of scheduling two individual sessions in one day, which many insurance companies will deny, consider planning one individual session and one family session). An additional way to decrease the cost for families is to include clinicians with lower fees than licensed psychologists/psychiatrists as part of the treatment team, including licensed clinical social workers/counselors and psychology trainees (e.g., postdoctoral fellows and externs). We provide an in-depth discussion of the training model and how this can be excellent for trainees, staff, and patients in Chapter 6. You may also consider being paneled on a select number of managed care plans, based on the most common plans in a given community and the quality of reimbursement. Alternatively, you may consider doing single-case agreements for select cases. However, keep in mind that the process of single-case agreements can be time consuming, and payments are not always timely once negotiations are complete.

Given the potential cost burden of a fee-for-service model, it is still helpful to plan and structure the clinical services the same way one would in a managed care model. The most common challenge in this regard is the number of services on a given day that can be billed to a managed care company by a single entity/individual. Many managed care companies will not pay for more than one service by the same provider in a single day. Spreading services across different days of the week usually avoids this issue. If more than one person is billing for different services on a given day, it is important to know if these are billed under the individual's tax ID number or the clinic's ID number. If the latter is the case, then there may be reimbursement issues. If a situation arises requiring more than one appointment in a given day, it is important to understand the billing implications before beginning to enroll patients.

Space

As discussed in Chapters 3 and 4, before embarking on development of an intensive treatment program, it is important to assess the space required for it and if these needs can be met. Depending on the format of your program, an intensive treatment program may require at least one group room along with an adequate number of breakout rooms for individual exposure work. Depending on program size, it may be helpful to have multiple group rooms, which allows for co-occurring groups of patient cohorts and possible parent groups. It is also important to understand the impact of a large group-based program on waiting room space when all the patients and parents arrive and depart and on the practice experience of any clinicians sharing the public spaces and group rooms in a practice. Another consideration related to space is whether there is adequate sound-proofing or whether white noise machines will provide adequate sound-proofing to allow for privacy and confidentiality during individual treatment meetings. Of course, depending on your setting, space requirements may impact infrastructure costs that should be considered before finalizing your intensive treatment constraints and beginning to recruit and enroll patients.

In summary, development and implementation of an intensive treatment program can pose a number of practical challenges that must be carefully considered before embarking on the process of starting an intensive program. While the topics covered in this chapter are not an exhaustive list of such considerations, they represent some of the most frequently encountered barriers that should be considered in the planning process. The process should include self-reflection on whether intensive work is the right fit for you and your team, the timing and schedule of your planned program, the fit within an existing patient population and community, and the type of practice environment in which you work. Careful consideration will optimize the experience of building such a program for the therapists, as well as the experience of the program for patients and families. Given the many ways to implement an intensive treatment program, we encourage you to consider creative implementation strategies, regardless of the challenges that your setting, institution, clinic, or regulatory bodies may pose.

CHAPTER 5 TAKE-HOME POINTS

- Understanding and anticipating challenges in advance will maximize your opportunity to problem solve and develop a successful treatment program.

- There are three different types of barriers and challenges that therapists should anticipate: (1) provider considerations, (2) consumer considerations, and (3) systems/infrastructure considerations.
- The planning and program-running process should include self-reflection on whether intensive work is the right fit for you and your team, the timing and schedule of your planned program, the fit with an existing patient population and community, and the type of practice environment in which you work.

Staffing Models and Training Opportunities

Staffing intensive treatment programs offers a myriad of excellent training opportunities that are ultimately mutually beneficial to the clinician in training, the institution or practice employing trainees, and the patients receiving care within a practice connected to a training program. Working with trainees who provide clinical hours as part of a supervised clinical placement and training program may make the treatment program more affordable for patients, as well as for the institution or practice setting. In this chapter, we describe the different staffing models for an intensive treatment program, including opportunities for working with trainees, and we offer examples of successful training models.

Intensive treatment for obsessive compulsive disorder (OCD) can be completed by any licensed mental health clinician with ample understanding of and experience with pediatric OCD and its evidence-based treatments. The staffing models selected for a given program will largely depend on the treatment setting, availability of well-trained clinicians, and budget for supporting clinicians' salaries. In a private practice setting, psychologists, social workers, or other licensed mental health professionals can offer intensive or condensed cognitive behavioral therapy (CBT) for OCD as solo practitioners or with a team of practitioners working together. In a university or academic medical center setting, intensive treatment programs will likely include some clinicians in training who are supervised by a licensed attending psychologist, psychiatrist, or other licensed clinician. We caution that each state has distinct regulations about the provision of supervision for trainee clinical hours, and that federal regulatory agencies and professional organizations have additional guidelines.

Working in an intensive treatment program offers a unique training opportunity to gain clinical experience with patients who have OCD and related conditions. The singular focus on OCD in such a program offers trainees the opportunity to develop an area of concentrated experience and work toward expertise in this area. Depending on the size of the program, if there is a group component, and how quickly patients are admitted and discharged, trainees in an intensive program may have the advantage of seeing many different patients and presentations in a short amount of time. During a 1-year clinical placement, a psychology trainee may gain experience with many more patients cycling through an intensive treatment program than is possible in a traditional weekly treatment training setting. This offers a wider range of exposure to OCD, such that the therapists in training will observe and work with a broad array of different OCD presentations and may gain further understanding of the complexity of comorbid depression, anxiety, tic disorders, and/or substance use.

The presence of clinical trainees within an intensive program is typically a cost-effective means for seeing more patients in a given program. This will reduce wait time for patients and, given the relatively lower stipends or salaries for graduate students, residents, and/or postdoctoral fellows relative to licensed clinicians, the ability to offer reduced fees to families in need. Having more therapists available to staff the many hours needed for intensive treatment also offers lower risk of clinician burnout. The mental health field also benefits from the dissemination of evidence-based care to the next generation of providers. This experience of teaching, training, and workforce development provides value to the field by expanding the number of therapists available with specialized training in the delivery of intensive exposure and response prevention (ERP) for OCD. It is critical that trainees receive strong and consistent supervision in their work to ensure that patients are receiving appropriate services and maximal benefit. Thus, inclusion of trainees in your intensive program will require that you supervise them appropriately from multiple perspectives, including legal, regulatory, payer, and training program guidelines.

A patient's exposure to multiple clinicians within an intensive treatment program may aid in the effectiveness of exposure practices and the generalization of treatment gains by introducing more variability into the exposure treatment process (Kircanski & Peris, 2015). These patients will have the opportunity to experience different clinical styles, and the patient will be more likely to "own" the change instead of overattributing change to one provider. In addition, with more clinicians available on the treatment team, it may facilitate more one-on-one attention for patients during the program, even in the context of a group program.

As is the case in all clinical training programs, patients must be made aware that they are working with a trainee and understand the structure for the trainee's clinical and administrative supervision. The patient and family should be informed of the frequency with which they may meet the trainee's supervisor and/or attending and the limits of confidentiality within trainee supervision. Often the supervisor or attending will see the patient together with the trainee for some portion of the treatment, at least initially or periodically, in order to best oversee the treatment plan and provision of good care. The patient should also be made aware of the timeline upon which the trainee's clinical rotation will end and whether this will impact the patient's care. Programs and institutions must also contend with the reality of trainee changeover, requiring a continued investment of teaching and training resources in new clinicians, and a less experienced group of new clinicians at the start of each training period that will require more oversight and guidance.

TRAINING MODELS AND CONSIDERATIONS

Whether the intensive treatment program will be staffed with trainees or entirely with licensed clinicians, the program administrators must set guidelines around the level and type of experience and prerequisite training required prior to starting work in an intensive OCD program. Mental health disciplines approach clinical training in different ways. Psychology doctoral programs with a clinical component (clinical psychology, counseling psychology, school psychology) typically begin formal clinical training in the first or second year of their programs. Students complete clinical rotations during their second, third, and sometimes later years of schooling, often at the same time as completing coursework and research requirements. The last stage of clinical training prior to acquisition of the doctoral degree for a psychologist is a predoctoral clinical internship, which is 1 year of intensive clinical training at a site outside of their academic program. Following the achievement of a doctoral degree, psychologists then complete another 1-year minimum of supervised clinical training hours to meet the requirements for licensure. Participation in an intensive treatment program could fulfill any stage of this clinical training and can aid in the accrual of a large number of clinical hours in a short period of time. Other clinical mental health specialists, such as social workers and mental health workers, will complete supervised clinical training as a part of their degree and licensing requirements.

Physicians training in psychiatry complete 4 years of medical school, during which time they participate in brief clinical clerkships to gain experience in a variety of medical departments and settings. The first year of postdegree clinical training is an internship followed by residency training in a specific discipline of medicine (psychiatry) and then advanced training in a clinical fellowship if desired (e.g., child psychiatry, forensic psychiatry). Residents and fellows in psychiatry can prescribe medicine and complete medical assessments, in addition to other clinical responsibilities in an intensive program, although we recommend this occur under the supervision of a psychiatrist with expertise in pharmacotherapy for pediatric OCD.

An intensive treatment program should have an in-depth orientation and minimum training requirement to ensure all trainees and licensed clinicians in the program, regardless of prior experience, are well versed in the phenomenology and presentation of OCD, as well as the evidence-based interventions employed within the program. In order to provide training in the component interventions of the program, training can include didactic teaching, assigned readings, discussion of case examples, and role-plays to rehearse the delivery of specific skills or practice managing a variety of clinical challenges. As is the case with many clinical approaches, the goal is for clinicians to demonstrate fidelity to the treatment model while being able to use component interventions flexibly. This flexible application of the model aims to best meet the needs of each patient during a given clinical encounter. An important part of on-the-job training that occurs in clinical training programs, including in intensive treatment programs, is the ability for trainees to observe more experienced clinicians live and additionally to be observed live by supervisors and other clinicians. The observations can then be discussed in clinical supervision meetings to allow for questions and feedback. Supervision can occur in a one-to-one meeting or in a group context with more than one clinician from the program. Individual supervision offers a more intimate setting for clinical learning and trainee development and disclosure. Group supervision provides a supportive context for learning from a cohort of people, providing access to learning from the patient encounters of peers and receiving feedback from multiple perspectives.

Trainees may have different schedules or allotted hours for clinical training, thus rotating trainees on different days may provide maximum coverage for patients and clinical exposure for trainees. The potential duration of the training experience or rotation in an intensive treatment program is broad; it could be 4 months, 6 months, 12 months, or longer. The duration of training should be determined so the time committed for training and supervision is worth the investment by the individual trainees and maximizes benefits to the program. The number of clinical contact hours in an intensive treatment program are often quite high and can be beneficial for those who are accruing hours toward licensure. It may be possible to complete a training experience in an intensive treatment program as well as training in other traditional outpatient sites, depending on the trainees' and the program's schedule. Often an intensive treatment program may offer daytime hours, which may help fill the schedule for trainees who are also seeing outpatients during later afternoon hours.

Each program setting may approach staffing and training needs differently. Teaching hospitals have many levels of trainees embedded in the system already, including residents, fellows, graduate student externs, pre- and postdegree interns, and postdoctoral fellows. A university setting is more likely to employ and train graduate students and may also utilize undergraduate volunteers. A private practice setting may offer training opportunities, such as a clinical apprenticeship, to accrue supervised clinical hours toward licensure. A clinical apprenticeship, externship, or postdoctoral fellowship in a private practice setting may provide lower cost options for patients, as well as earn additional income for the practice. Some programs may employ "behavioral technicians" or behavioral specialists, who have typically completed a bachelor- or master's-level education and then completed focused training in the provision of behavior therapy and exposure-based treatment. In order to utilize a behavioral technician model of staffing, there must be a plan in place for a prerequisite level of education and experiences and a system for training in exposure therapy within the program. Again, professional guidelines and regulations/laws imposed by systems, states, and payers will apply.

There are other staffing models that do not require a training component, including utilizing multiple licensed providers within a group practice to staff an intensive treatment program. The collaboration with other providers already embedded in the practice will help alleviate too much clinical burden on any one practitioner and allow the program and patients to benefit from the expertise of multiple providers. Therapists with different training backgrounds may also be able to fulfill different roles within the program, such as exposure practice, medication management, patient triage, and/or family sessions.

Given the complexity of OCD as a condition, and the nuances of successful exposure therapy, training in ERP requires close supervision, particularly for patients who may be at risk of emotional escalation and/or impulsive or unsafe behaviors. Therapists with less experience may need to shadow more experienced therapists or obtain live supervision for a period of time before independent practice begins. A plan for managing risky or potentially harmful patient behaviors must be in place and clearly communicated to all staff, regardless of role or level of training. In any program with multiple providers, a model for communication between staff members to promote continuity of care is necessary. This can include verbal handoffs, chart notes, or other means of communication between team members. There is a great deal of variability and flexibility in staffing an intensive treatment program. These choices, including financial decisions, should be made with the goal of offering the best possible clinical care and, in some models, the most effective educational opportunities for trainees.

CHAPTER 6 TAKE-HOME POINTS

- Intensive treatment programs offer unique training opportunities that are ultimately mutually beneficial to the therapist in training, the institution or practice employing trainees, and the patients receiving care within a practice connected to a training program.
- Working with trainees who provide clinical hours as part of a supervised clinical placement and training program may make the treatment program more affordable for patients.
- The singular focus on OCD in such a program offers trainees an opportunity to develop an area of concentrated experience and work toward expertise in this area.
- It is critical that trainees receive strong and consistent supervision in their work in order to ensure that patients are receiving appropriate services and maximal benefit.

Treatment Pathway:
From Referral to Aftercare

The treatment process has multiple phases, starting with the first phone call between your program and the prospective patient and ending with when the patient is comfortably situated with an aftercare plan. Intensive treatment can be very beneficial, but it is not the right fit for everyone. Careful screening at the first point of contact can help triage families and ensure that they reach the appropriate treatment and setting quickly. Often a brief initial phone screen will be followed by a thorough in-person intake assessment that allows for a deeper evaluation of obsessive compulsive disorder (OCD), comorbid conditions, and treatment readiness. Such an evaluation can help shape the treatment plan and match it to individual patient and family needs. During the active treatment phase, the all-important process of symptom reduction occurs, with regular (e.g., weekly) symptom monitoring in order to both track treatment progress *and* allow the treatment team and family to work together toward a transition to a less restrictive care setting (e.g., once- or twice-weekly outpatient). During this transition, tapering the frequency of sessions and creating a supportive discharge plan will allow families to maintain their gains long term. This chapter details each phase of the treatment process and discusses how to set up each of these phases for success.

PHASE 1: SCREENING

A relatively brief preadmission screening with parents by phone or email can be a useful step toward determining whether a particular intensive treatment program is a good fit for a family. An initial screening can serve to manage referrals without spending unnecessary time with queries from families who are not good candidates for intensive treatment, in general or for a particular program. As part of the screening, information regarding the treatment program is provided to families, and information about the potential patient and family is obtained as well. Information that is valuable to provide to the family initially includes, but may not be limited to:

- Location
- Fees (including self-pay and insurance options)
- Treatment format (e.g., group and/or individual)
- Treatment scheduling (days and times of treatment)
- Typical duration of treatment
- Commitment required of patient and caregiver(s)

Depending on the type of services offered and comorbidities addressed, the screen may also be an opportunity to provide information about whether your program has requirements about minimum length of treatment that a family must agree to in order to participate.

In addition to age and other basic identifying information, additional information that can be collected from the parent or caregiver as part of a screening process includes the following:

- **Treatment history:** The importance of collecting treatment history relates to whether the potential patient has had an appropriate trial of outpatient exposure and response prevention (ERP). If there has not been a previous trial, a reasonable consideration might be whether once weekly (i.e., nonintensive treatment) might be sufficient before considering intensive treatment.
- **Current symptoms and their related impairments:** Although a brief screening is not designed to be a diagnostic evaluation (as discussed below), collecting symptom information can help determine whether (1) OCD seems to be of sufficient intensity to warrant admission and (2) whether other symptoms that are contraindicated for intensive treatment are present. Specifically, impulsivity, aggression, self-harm, low distress tolerance, and emotional dysregulation, although problematic for ERP in any setting, may be more difficult to deal with when delivering ERP in an intensive format due to the rigorous schedule of exposures. It may also be important to ask screening questions about impairment and domains of functioning. For example, if the patient successfully participates in school and extracurricular activities and the family would be unwilling to stop those activities because they occur on the same days/times as treatment, this may be an indicator that traditional weekly outpatient treatment may be more appropriate or that intensive treatment during a scheduled break from academics and extracurriculars (e.g., summer break) could be a better fit in regard to timing.
- **Consent and motivation:** Although laws vary from state to state, in general, adolescents cannot be treated without their assent or consent. More importantly, beyond legal concerns, ERP treatment for OCD treatment is not effective without considerable effort and motivation on the part of the patient. For these reasons, even at the screening process, it is recommended to collect information regarding whether the child

or adolescent has agreed to (or at least been informed about) the plan to pursue treatment.

PHASE 2: INTAKE ASSESSMENT

After a triage screening, many programs require an additional in-depth assessment prior to accepting a patient for admission. One of the primary purposes of this additional step is to gather more complete information regarding the diagnostic "picture" of the child or adolescent. This may be done using an unstructured clinical interview or, preferably, with a semistructured clinical interview, such as the Anxiety Disorders Interview Schedule (ADIS; Silverman & Albano, 1996). In addition, given that it is useful in subsequent treatment efforts, many programs assess for specific information about OCD symptoms at this time, using a gold-standard clinician-rated instrument such as the Children's Yale Brown Obsessive Compulsive Scale (CYBOCS; Scahill et al., 1997). Before undertaking such an assessment, it is helpful to provide brief psychoeducation about OCD to better allow the family to respond to questions about obsessions and compulsions. If it becomes clear by the end of this intake assessment that your intensive setting would be an appropriate fit and the family appears to be initially motivated to participate, providing a brief tour of the treatment setting space may reduce the patient's initial concerns about the first day of treatment.

While the presence of comorbid conditions can complicate the use of ERP to treat OCD in general, we consider below how particular comorbid conditions and/or symptoms can be specifically affected by intensive ERP treatment and how to plan and sequence treatment should they arise in the intake assessment.

Depression: Major depressive disorder (MDD) is a very common comorbidity with OCD. An important consideration when MDD is present is whether the depression is a separate primary problem warranting immediate intervention, or secondary to the OCD presentation in that it is a consequence of feeling hopeless and sad because living with OCD has become so difficult for the patient. This distinction is important because, if depression symptoms are primary or co-primary with OCD, the mood symptoms, irritability, or anhedonia may affect motivation and thus interfere with engagement in treatment. In this case, you might consider referring the patient to treatment for the depression symptoms prior to the start of OCD-specific treatment. If depression symptoms are secondary to distress caused by OCD symptoms, they are less likely to interfere with OCD treatment, and the individual may be more motivated to work on OCD treatment due to the promise of future improvement in the depression symptoms.

Autism spectrum disorder (ASD) and neurodevelopmental considerations: The evaluation of ASD is important in considering the possible differential diagnosis. While the symptoms can look similar, sometimes a diagnosis of ASD may better capture the patient's symptoms and clinical picture than OCD does. Alternatively, ASD may present as truly comorbid with OCD. While it is certainly possible and common to treat OCD in a patient who also has ASD, frequently it requires changes to the treatment approach. Since groups are commonly incorporated into intensive treatment programs, it should be considered whether the ASD symptoms will affect the patient's ability to function well in a group setting and whether the patient has sufficient distress tolerance to withstand the increased distress that comes with the demand of multiple exposures per day and week. Similarly, patients with other neurodevelopmental conditions such as significant intellectual disability or cognitive delays may have difficulties with understanding the treatment model or managing the pace of intensive treatment. The treatment may need to be slowed so that such patients do not feel overly dysregulated or upset.

Oppositional defiant disorder (ODD): Children and adolescents with ODD and other behavioral issues do not tend to do well with intensive treatment because they are generally noncompliant with tasks that are challenging, uncomfortable, or unwanted. By definition, ERP requires a patient to regularly engage in facing unwanted, uncomfortable tasks. In these cases, the concern may not be isolated to intensive treatment and can be the case for weekly ERP as well. Given that compliance is often higher for exposures that occur during treatment sessions (vs. at home), intensive treatment shouldn't necessarily be ruled out for patients with ODD. Care should be taken to avoid adding battles over exposure homework in consideration of the family's other struggles. Additionally, given that families of patients with ODD often need extensive parent- and family-based work, it may be difficult to focus solely on OCD and not be distracted in treatment by the other issues that are present. If the patient is unable to fully participate in treatment, consider sequencing treatment for ODD first to ensure readiness for engagement in targeted OCD treatment.

Attention-deficit/hyperactivity disorder (ADHD): If patients present with ADHD symptoms that are well managed, they may be ready to engage in intensive treatment for OCD. For those with an ADHD presentation that is not under the control of either a rigorous behavior plan or medication, intensive treatment is not recommended due to the difficulty that such patients may have with longer sessions. Including more frequent breaks and clear transitions back to tasks may be helpful even for those patients whose symptoms are well managed by medication.

In the presence of all co-occurring disorders, one should consider sequencing treatment. That is, the family may need to receive treatment for another condition prior to OCD treatment (e.g., parent management training for ODD or cognitive behavioral therapy [CBT] for MDD) and then return for intensive treatment for OCD.

PHASE 3: ACTIVE TREATMENT

Section III of this guidebook includes treatment component content. Here, we highlight that symptom assessment throughout treatment is necessary. A clear symptom and diagnostic assessment at the initial intake session/start of treatment is imperative to treatment success, but this assessment is merely the first of many.

Throughout treatment, it is important to reassess symptoms via multiple methods to ensure that treatment is progressing and to guide when to taper treatment to a less intensive frequency. Reassessing OCD symptoms using the CYBOCS is a helpful way to gain perspective on symptoms, impairment, and patient control over symptoms, and it can also allow for feedback to the patient and family about improvement or areas that need more work. In addition to formal measures, rerating a patient's hierarchy or challenge list can similarly inform which symptoms and targets have responded to treatment and which need additional focus and attention. When assessing for OCD symptoms and severity, consider interfering factors: comorbidity that may be interfering with progress, family factors that may be contributing to symptoms, and any challenges with treatment engagement. These periodic assessments will allow you to address any interfering factors and target remaining symptoms in a systematic way. We have included the OCD Home-Based Symptom Assessment in the Appendix, which may be a useful tool.

The frequency of ongoing assessments will depend on the setup of your program. For some programs and patients, weekly assessment with the above-described tools may be helpful. For other programs, the CYBOCS might be completed every 2 or 4 weeks. We advise that the exposure hierarchy and patient/parent monitoring forms be reviewed and incorporated as part of the homework review at the start of each treatment day, and, of course, assessment of patient reactions to exposures using distress ratings and behavioral observation occurs on a moment-to-moment basis during exposures.

When a patient has achieved many or most impairing treatment targets, or when the patient reaches responder or remission status, you can discuss and consider whether it makes sense to taper treatment, as described below. While the specific goal may vary by patient and family, a 25% reduction in CYBOCS scores may indicate treatment response, and 45%–50% reduction, or a score of 14 or below, may indicate symptom remission (Storch, Lewin, et al., 2010).

PHASE 4: TREATMENT TAPER

We highly encourage tapering treatment in anticipation of discharge to a less intensive level of care. It is exciting and rewarding when patients meet their treatment goals and show rapid improvement, yet it is important to recognize that the intensive treatment setting is very supportive, and families may struggle to continue making strides without the intensive level of support. The ultimate goal in the intensive treatment context is to provide patients and families with skills that result in symptom reduction that allow for patients to continue to thrive once they step down from the intensive level of care. Tapering sessions to a lower frequency near the end of intensive treatment has both clinical and logistical benefits.

Tapering sessions and giving patients "off days" allows you to observe patients' progress when they have more space and time between each session. This is an assessment opportunity during which you can see how well patients maintain independent exposure practices and how they manage the added stress of returning to daily life, which may include extracurriculars, increased homework, or higher expectations for independence. If a patient is able to maintain a low level of OCD symptoms and consistently displays the ability to fight urges to give in to obsessions and compulsions, this is a great indicator that the patient may be ready to graduate from the intensive level of care. This not only is helpful for the therapist but can boost patients' and parents' confidence about lowering the level of active support. Alternatively, some patients struggle when they begin a treatment taper, and this, too, can inform the treatment course. Observing this allows a provider to identify the barriers to independent practice and maintenance of gains and then provide tools to overcome these barriers. This process may include teaching patients to take more ownership of independent exposure practice, stress management, shifting rewards program, increasing family involvement, and discussions of how to integrate exposures and treatment strategies into a rich, full life that includes school, extracurricular activities, and social connections.

A treatment taper may also provide some logistical benefits: if insurance will no longer cover daily sessions or puts a limit on how many remaining sessions it will cover, tapering to a lower frequency stretches the remaining sessions over a longer period of time to allow patients to gradually step down from the intensive level of care. Similarly, if a family is paying costs directly, when a patient is thriving, the family may not need to pay for sessions at the same frequency or intensity that was initially indicated. Tapering frequency may allow for lower per-week costs. Finally, families who have traveled to·participate in an intensive program may have specific dates by which they need to return home to a location without access to intensive treatment. For these families, tapering will allow that transition to go smoothly as it gradually steps the patient down from intensive care to the level they will be receiving upon return home.

The transition out of intensive treatment programs starts at the beginning of treatment. When a patient enters an intensive treatment program, assess what the potential aftercare plans might be available. Some patients arrive having previously seen a highly trained outpatient provider who can continue the work that the patient is doing on discharge from your program. Others have a therapist that they'd like to return to, but it is unclear whether the therapist they previously worked with is trained in OCD treatment. Some families don't yet have an aftercare plan and have been struggling to figure out how to manage outpatient care or have not considered it at all due to the severity of symptoms. Finally, there will be patients who do not need regular weekly therapy upon discharge and may benefit more from information on how to maintain gains independently and return for booster sessions if needed.

For families previously in treatment with a well-trained OCD provider, communication with existing providers prior to a patient starting intensive treatment and throughout intensive treatment will allow for a seamless transition out of your program and back to the original provider. Understanding the treatment targets that the patient had been working on prior to coming to your program will inform the treatment course, and communicating new gains, strategies, and what has (and has not!) worked for a specific patient and family will allow the existing provider to continue treatment in a way that best meets the patient's needs. If possible, cross-tapering can be highly beneficial: as patients decrease time in the intensive program, they can begin sessions with their aftercare provider. However, not all insurers allow a cross-taper, so this should be discussed with the family well in advance. Additionally, a cross-taper is unlikely to be allowed if the intensive program exists within a bundled service, such as within a partial hospital program or intensive outpatient program setting.

Other families may start intensive treatment after previously working with a provider who is not well versed in ERP. These providers may have a very important role in the patient's and family's life, which is important to understand and respect. In this scenario, it is important to communicate with the family and provider to determine how the patient and family will maintain ERP gains once the patient is discharged from your program. Facilitating a referral to a local OCD specialist in lieu of or in conjunction with the existing provider will be helpful, and navigating how the patient will manage this aftercare plan should begin during the active intensive treatment phase.

Many families do not have a set plan of how to maintain treatment gains once they graduate from intensive treatment. This can be because they were not happy with their previous providers, they are new to treatment, or they live in areas where treatment is difficult to access. Researching which providers will be able to help the patient and family maintain ERP gains early on in treatment is essential. Many providers have wait-lists, or it may be challenging to find a provider at all, and identifying these barriers will allow you to troubleshoot them. Further, once the aftercare provider is identified, communication throughout treatment will boost the chances for a successful transition on discharge. For families that are struggling to find a local aftercare provider, telehealth can be an excellent option that allows families to access continued evidence-based care with a provider who is a great fit, even when care is not available locally.

For patients who no longer need active care upon discharge, it is still helpful to find a local provider who can provide booster sessions if needed. For these families, communicate when and how to contact a provider for support and emphasize that asking for a booster session or short-term support does *not* reflect a setback. On the contrary, asking for a booster session can be a sign of strength; knowing when and how to ask for support from a provider is a skill in and of itself.

Once an aftercare provider is identified and consistent communication with the provider is in place, the focus can be on the patient's transition out of intensive treatment. This can be a challenging time for many patients and families, given that intensive treatment can be a transformative experience that has brought them from highly impaired to fully functioning in a short period of time. The end of treatment should focus heavily on maintenance and relapse prevention and building a patient's ability to practice, maintain, and apply skills independently. Chapter 14 details maintenance and relapse prevention strategies, including teaching patients to be their own therapists, writing themselves letters to remind them of core skills and support, and ways to tackle challenging barriers that may interfere with maintaining success.

This chapter largely has focused on patients for whom intensive treatment *is* the right fit, yet, even with thoughtful screening and thorough evaluation, some patients will begin intensive treatment and find that it is not the right level of care. If this is the case, having a discussion with families about the right level of care, and helping them access it, can be the most beneficial intervention. Some patients will opt for more standard weekly outpatient care. Others may find that intensive treatment in an outpatient setting is insufficient and seek partial hospitalization or residential programs. For others, OCD is present, but there are interfering comorbidities that need to be addressed first, and a program that can provide care for the comorbidity may be a better fit.

CHAPTER 7 TAKE-HOME POINTS

- The treatment process has multiple phases, starting with the first phone call between your program and the prospective patient and ending with when the patient is comfortably situated with an aftercare plan.
- Intensive treatment can be very beneficial, but it is not the right fit for everyone.
- Phase 1: Screening: This brief phase can help assess appropriateness for a treatment program prior to having a family complete a full intake assessment.
- Phase 2: Intake Assessment: The intake assessment will allow you to fully assess OCD symptoms and possible comorbid conditions using standardized measures. It will also allow you to get to know the patient and family. This phase will determine acceptance to your program and will provide valuable information and education to the provider as well as the family.
- Phase 3: Active Treatment: This is where treatment takes place! We detail many treatment elements in Section III of this guidebook.
- Phase 4: Treatment Taper: While this is listed as the fourth phase, it is imperative to begin planning for the end of treatment from day one. Consider tapering treatment as a way to transition out of intensive treatment, and to assess how gains are maintained with less support.

Medication in the Context of an Intensive Treatment Program

In obsessive compulsive disorder (OCD) treatment, questions about medications are inevitable, including the role of medications in OCD treatment, sequencing of treatment, the interaction of medications with intensive treatment, medication dosing, and duration of medication treatment. We have found that successful intensive treatment requires that therapists be able to answer these questions within the scope of their professional training, and that close collaboration with psychiatrists ensures that patients receive the most effective treatments, that accurate information is being shared with patients, and that medication decisions do not inadvertently impact the exposure and response prevention (ERP) work in negative ways. In this chapter, we review some of the most common medication-related topics that come up in the context of an intensive treatment program.

There are particular medication-related questions that frequently come up during the intake process, when families are trying to decide if intensive treatment is right for them and how to think about the different treatment options available. One of the most frequently asked questions is whether families should wait to start medication until they have first tried the ERP aspects of the intensive treatment program. The answer to this question is very individualized but should be based on the existing literature examining the effectiveness of ERP, medications, or the combination of the two.

The first-line medical treatment for pediatric OCD are the selective serotonin reuptake inhibitors (SSRIs), along with the tricyclic antidepressant clomipramine. Studies examining the efficacy of SSRIs compared to placebo for the treatment of pediatric OCD are universally positive, including trials of sertraline, fluoxetine, fluvoxamine, and paroxetine (Geller et al., 2001, 2004; March et al., 1998; POTS Team, 2004; Riddle et al., 2001). This was further supported by a meta-analysis, which found highly significant differences in efficacy between SSRIs and placebo (Geller et al., 2003).

It is perhaps more important for therapists delivering ERP to understand what the research tells us about the differential efficacy of ERP and medications. The two seminal studies to date examining the role of ERP, medications (SSRIs), or combination therapy for pediatric OCD are the Pediatric OCD Treatment Study (POTS I) and the follow-up POTS II trial. These trials refer to cognitive behavioral therapy (CBT) to include ERP, so we have referred to the treatment as CBT here.

The POTS I trial studied the efficacy of CBT alone, sertraline alone, and the combination of CBT and sertraline. The study indicated that, while CBT alone and sertraline alone were effective (Cohen's d of 0.97 and 0.67, respectively), the combination of CBT plus sertraline was significantly more effective, with a very large effect size (Cohen's $d = 1.40$). It's important to also understand that there were significant site effects found in POTS. At one site, very large effect sizes were found for CBT alone (1.6) and combined treatment (1.5) versus a moderate effect size (0.53) for sertraline alone. At a second site, these effect sizes were 0.51, 1.29, and 0.8, respectively. Thus, combined treatment appeared less vulnerable than CBT alone to differences in outcome related to treatment setting/site. The POTS team concluded that patients with pediatric OCD should begin treatment either with CBT alone or with a combination of CBT and an SSRI (POTS Team, 2004).

The POTS II trial compared the effectiveness of augmenting existing SSRI treatment with full CBT or basic instruction in CBT. Subjects were previous partial responders to an adequate trial of an SSRI and remained on the SSRI for the duration of the POTS II trial. This study found that augmentation with full CBT was superior to either continued medication management alone or augmentation with basic instruction in CBT, demonstrating the importance of providing full CBT by an experienced therapist (Franklin et al., 2011). The Child-Adolescent Multimodal Study (CAMS), the largest, most rigorous such study to date for non-OCD pediatric anxiety disorders, found very similar results, with combination treatment superior to either sertraline or CBT alone and all treatments better than placebo (Walkup et al., 2008). In addition, a meta-analysis showed that the effect sizes of CBT alone (Cohen's $d = 1.2$) and CBT with an SSRI (Cohen's $d = 1.7$) were both larger than an SSRI alone (Cohen's $d = 0.75$), indicating that CBT was more effective than medication treatment alone (Sánchez-Meca et al., 2014).

MEDICATION QUESTIONS AND DECISION MAKING IN INTENSIVE TREATMENT

The primary questions for therapists and medication providers are how to synthesize the evidence base to help counsel patients about the role of medication, ERP, or the combination of the two and how to think about sequencing them. Incorporating what we know from the literature and the recommendations of current practice parameters, the first consideration is the severity of a patient's OCD (Geller & March, 2012). If the patient is treatment naïve, has mild-to-moderate OCD, and is considering intensive treatment in an effort to do a more condensed treatment, for instance over a school break, then it would be reasonable to start with ERP without medication. For patients with moderate-to-severe OCD and/or OCD that has not responded to prior trials of ERP alone, we strongly recommend that patients receive combination treatment with an SSRI and ERP, rather than waiting to see if ERP alone will work. An additional reason to recommend patients begin an SSRI, instead of waiting to see how things progress in the intensive program is the length of time it takes for medications to work. Patients should not expect the medication to take effect for 3 to 4 weeks from the time they achieve a given dose, and, given that it takes time to reach the optimal dose, it may take up to 6 months for the full effect. By waiting to see if ERP alone works or fails, patients lose precious time. This time, and the frustration that can come with time passing without significant improvement, may lead to the false belief that ERP is not effective, when in fact it may have been effective in combination with the medication.

Frequent follow-up questions may arise at any time during the intensive treatment process, including dosing of medications, how long to expect to be on medication, side effects, and use of medications to relieve acute anxiety ahead of anxiety-provoking exposures. For a highly detailed exploration of these questions, some of which are beyond the scope of this book, we recommend a skilled psychopharmacologist, especially when considering the nuances of medication side effects and specific dosing questions. It is, however, important to understand the overarching principles, even as a nonprescribing clinician, in order to both educate patients and ensure they are not unnecessarily receiving conflicting information.

There is tremendous confusion and mythology among both the general public and clinicians about the dosing of medications for pediatric OCD and anxiety. This, again, is a place where an understanding of the clinical trial literature can provide reliable guidelines that can be used to educate families and reassure them. Nonprescribers often play a key role by helping patients and families understand the rationale for medication dosing and ensuring that families do not receive conflicting information. In our experience, the most common misconception is that children and adolescents should be on only small doses of medications. This is true of many medications for children in other domains (e.g., weight-based dosing of antibiotics) but is not true of the most common and best studied medications for treatment of pediatric OCD, namely, the SSRIs. In the POTS trial, the mean highest daily dose of sertraline was 133 mg. The median dose of sertraline in the group who received combination therapy (CBT + sertraline) was 150 mg daily, while for those who received sertraline alone it was 200 mg (POTS Team, 2004). These are robust doses toward the top of the dose range approved by the Food and Drug Administration (FDA) for sertraline for both adults and children (200 mg daily). In practice, providers who treat OCD find they sometimes must use doses above the FDA-approved maximum. The CAMS trial found similar results with regard to dosing for non-OCD anxiety disorders, with a mean final dose of 133.7 mg daily in the combination treatment (CBT + sertraline) group and 146 mg daily in the sertraline-only group (Walkup et al., 2008). The table below provides a guideline for dosing to help therapists understand the dose ranges they may encounter.

Medication Dosing Guidelines

MEDICATION (BRAND NAME)	STARTING DOSE CHILDREN (MG)	STARTING DOSE ADOLESCENTS (MG)	TYPICAL DOSE RANGE (MG)
Citalopram (Celexa)	2.5–10	10–20	10–60
Escitalopram (Lexapro)	2.5–5	5–10	10–30
Fluoxetine (Prozac)[a]	5–10	10–20	20–80
Fluvoxamine (Luvox)[a]	12.5–25	25–50	50–300
Paroxetine (Paxil)	2.5–10	10	20–60
Sertraline (Zoloft)[a]	12.5–25	25–50	50–200
Clomipramine (Anafranil)[a]	6.25–25	25	50–200

[a]Approved by the FDA for OCD in children and adolescents.
Adapted from the American Academy of Child and Adolescent Psychiatry "Practice Parameter for the Assessment and Treatment of Children and Adolescents With Obsessive-Compulsive Disorder" (2012. Updated to include escitalopram.

It is important for therapists working in an intensive treatment program to understand that these seemingly "high" doses of SSRIs are the norm and are supported by the literature. Providing adequate education about dosing helps families understand this, may increase their comfort with a prescribed treatment plan, or allow them to self-advocate with a medication provider. A more detailed discussion about dosing should be referred back to the treating psychiatrist.

Another common question is about taking "rescue," "PRN," or "as needed" medications before engaging in exposures, both in the program and at home, hoping that reducing acute anxiety with these medications will reduce distress and increase success during exposures. While we sympathize with patients and understand that ERP is inherently uncomfortable, it is important to remember that a key component to successful ERP is riding the wave of distress and anxiety, letting it crest, and experiencing the resolution of the distress after completing the exposure (see Chapter 11 for details). Short-circuiting this process with anxiolytic medication ahead of the exposure inactivates the key component of ERP. This is consistent with the theory of exposure therapy and our knowledge of the components of CBT that are most important for treatment response in OCD. Additionally, preclinical animal research has found that benzodiazepines (BZDs) interfere with the extinction learning required for successful exposure-based treatment (Bouton et al., 1990; Bustos et al., 2009; Hart et al., 2014). While more research in clinical samples is required, these preclinical data suggest that clinicians should think carefully about using BZDs during exposure-based treatments. In our collective work and that of close colleagues in other intensive programs, we do not recommend use of these medications in treatment sessions.

Finally, patients frequently want to know how long they will need to stay on medication. Unfortunately, to date there is not a single study examining discontinuation of medications for pediatric OCD, anxiety disorders, or depression. Most often, it is recommended that patients stay on their SSRI for at least 1 year from the time their symptoms go into remission or are in good control. This is based on adult literature and practice guidelines (American Psychiatric Association et al., 2007; Koran & Simpson, 2013). It is important that patients understand that OCD is usually a chronic illness with a waxing and waning course. As a result they should not stop medication too quickly after an initial positive response, and there is a reasonable chance that they will have a return of OCD symptoms as the dose is decreased. It is also possible that, even if they do not have an immediate return of symptoms, they may have a recurrence of symptoms in the future. The specifics of any dose reduction should be under the guidance of the patient's treating physician. In general terms, the dose reduction should be very slow with at least 1 month, preferably 2 months, between dose reductions to adequately monitor for symptom recurrence. If the patient is participating in ongoing CBT during the reduction, it is a good idea to continue that exposure-based work. If the patient is not in active CBT treatment, it is often recommended to schedule some booster sessions of CBT during the dose reduction to help address any emergent OCD symptoms. These booster sessions may allow for control of the OCD symptoms without requiring the dose to be increased back to the last effective dose. They also allow for closer monitoring of changes during the discontinuation phase of treatment. We do not recommend that patients begin tapering medications while still completing an intensive treatment program, though it is perfectly reasonable for a physician to make changes to medication during an intensive program based on adequacy of response or tolerability issues.

These are the most common questions that we find arise about medications in our intensive treatment programs, but it is far from a complete accounting of possible questions. An exhaustive review of the medical treatment options and their considerations is beyond the scope of this book. Therapists are encouraged to collaborate closely with patients' prescribers to optimize treatment and prevent misunderstandings.

CHAPTER 8 TAKE-HOME POINTS

- In OCD treatment, questions about medications are inevitable. Successful intensive treatment requires that therapists be able to answer these questions within the scope of their professional training.
- Close collaboration with psychiatrists better ensures that patients receive the most effective treatments, that accurate information is being shared with patients, and that medication decisions do not inadvertently impact the ERP work in negative ways.

- The combination of CBT and SSRIs is superior to either an SSRI or CBT alone, and all treatments are better than placebo.
- One of the most common misconceptions is that children and adolescents should be on only small doses of medications. This is true of many medications for children in other domains (e.g., weight-based dosing of antibiotics), but it is not true of the most common and best studied medications for treatment of pediatric OCD, namely, the SSRIs.
- Providing adequate education about dosing helps families understand this, may increase their comfort with a prescribed treatment plan, or allow them to self-advocate with a medication provider. A more detailed discussion about dosing should be referred back to the treating psychiatrist.

Treating a Child Requires Treating the Family and Community

The treatment of patients with obsessive compulsive disorder (OCD) often requires the inclusion of parents, broader family members, or other important people in the patient's daily life (e.g., other caregivers, teachers, close friends). This is particularly true for the effective treatment of children and adolescents with OCD, where the inclusion of parents or other close family members is paramount to optimize treatment outcomes (Peris et al., 2017). Trusted family members or close friends are often asked or compelled to participate in compulsions or anxiety-driven behaviors in order to alleviate distress for the individual with OCD, and these behaviors are just as important to address as the compulsions that the individual performs. For example, a family member who has touched something perceived to be dirty or contaminated by the patient with OCD may be asked to, or feel the need to, wash their hands in order to allay the patient's distress, even if the family member does not struggle with contamination concerns. Parents may adapt the home environment to avoid OCD triggers in an attempt to avoid upsetting their child or disrupting the family routine. They may unknowingly participate in a ritual that then becomes a frequently repeated process. These cycles can create conflict, confusion, and high emotions within a family system, thus requiring a family component to treatment in order to optimize treatment outcome.

Parental accommodation of or participation in OCD and anxiety-driven behaviors is borne out of parents' innate drive to protect their children from distress or harm. It may be driven by parents' own distress or anxiety and/or observing the level of distress OCD symptoms are causing for children. Some parents fear that an intense experience of anxiety is harmful for their children. Others may have or have had OCD themselves and thus identify with the distress associated with obsessions and compulsions and, as a result, participate in rituals as a misguided attempt to help the child with the symptom burden. In other cases, the repetitive and compulsive behaviors associated with OCD interrupt and delay the child's and families' daily activities and routines, so parents may give in to OCD-related demands in an attempt to keep family life moving as smoothly as possible. As is the case with OCD symptoms, repeated participation often makes the frequency and/or scope of the compulsion greater, so over time parents then find themselves stuck in a pattern of OCD behaviors that is much more problematic than when it first began. Understanding the perspective of parents, and approaching parent and family work with compassion, understanding, and without judgment, is key to helping parents untangle the OCD web within their family.

In an intensive treatment program, the process of parent or family participation can be structured in a variety of ways. Primary caregivers should always be included in the intake process for youth under 18 (and in most circumstances should provide collateral information for young adult patients with the patient's permission). In intensive treatment programs that don't include groups, sessions may be reserved for parent sessions, family sessions, or joint sessions for the patient to be joined by their participating family member(s). In group programs, there can be separate group sessions for parents, siblings, or family members, with content tailored to the specific group. Generally, these individual or group sessions should include psychoeducation about OCD so the family members understand the symptoms and behaviors associated with OCD, with particular effort to reduce family confusion, conflict, blame, and stigma. Time and attention should be spent on specifically reducing family participation in rituals and/or accommodation of OCD-related behaviors. This may include distress tolerance and emotion regulation skills so parents and family members can manage their own emotions to best support their child or family member who is in exposure-based treatment. A clear explanation of the rationale, theoretical underpinnings, and process of exposure and response prevention (ERP) is essential.

Early in treatment, parental monitoring of how OCD symptoms interfere at home will help supplement the initial intake assessment and contribute to the overall treatment plan. This process also helps parents to understand the many and varied ways that OCD symptoms present in daily life. These concrete examples contribute to a comprehensive exposure hierarchy. Parents or others involved may contribute to adding compulsions or other behaviors to the exposure hierarchy and can be included in facilitating and/or rewarding the completion of at-home/between-session exposure practices as appropriate. During the treatment process, parents can learn what coping skills their children are learning in treatment in order to best support their children in using these skills at home and also when to refrain from using certain coping skills, such as during an exposure practice at home. Sessions with the patient and family member together may facilitate communication around exposure practices, and it may be helpful for parents to join an exposure session at some point in treatment to observe the exposure process in action and learn from the therapist how to best help the patient tolerate distress and complete the exposure exercise. In fact, for younger children, parents may be involved in much of the exposure treatment because they will be expected to facilitate their young child's between-session practice. Similarly, for youth of any age whose symptoms involve other family members (e.g., patient cannot touch, hug, or be near parent due to aggressive obsessions about causing physical harm), those family members may be incorporated into the exposure hierarchy and sub-sequently participate in many in- and between-session exposures.

Parent and family sessions may include a supportive component as well. In a group context, parents may appreciate getting to know other parents who are having similar experiences at home related to OCD. Siblings may benefit from learning more about OCD and its treatment to provide a context for stressful situations they witness or experience at home. Caregivers will likely have many questions to ask and emotions to express throughout the treatment process. Logistical considerations of how to manage the condensed or intensive treatment structure should be discussed early in the assessment and treatment process, in-cluding any issues related to insurance coverage, payment for the treatment, and travel considerations if the treatment program is far from their home. As the treatment progresses and with increasing focus as the treatment nears its end, parents should be included to discuss maintenance of gains, relapse prevention, and how the home environment may change and continue to adapt as the OCD symptoms are less present or time consuming. A discussion with parents about early warning signs that OCD symptoms may be returning or worsening is key prior to discharge from treatment. Parents should be included in the discussion of the follow-up treatment plan for the patient, and a separate referral for treatment for a parent or other family members may be warranted for continued support and/or separate individual or family treatment as indicated.

For patients, it is often helpful to include a teacher or other important figure in the child's life who may benefit from understanding the role of OCD and ERP in the child's daily functioning. Teachers, school counselors, or other school per-sonnel provide an important perspective during the intake process to have a full understanding of how OCD symptoms impact important spheres of develop-ment. Similarly, some teachers, coaches, or other important community leaders may be able to support ongoing exposures and reduce avoidance or accommoda-tion of anxiety if they have a good understanding of the treatment and home prac-tice plan. These contacts must only be made with the consent of the patient and parents. The contact can be made through collateral phone calls, having teachers fill out symptom questionnaires or other structured reports on the patient's functioning, sending treatment handouts via email or through the family, and/or discussing ways that all important adults can facilitate elements of the treatment plan in home, school, and other settings. In addition, the therapist may want to contact some teachers or other adults in the patient's life because they have signif-icant misperceptions about OCD and therefore have done or said things that are unhelpful to the patient, particularly during the treatment process. Again, con-sent of patient and parents is required.

Separate manuals exist for family-focused OCD treatment (e.g., Freeman & Garcia, 2009; Peris & Piacentini, 2016), which provide comprehensive details on parent and family interventions for OCD. Parent and family work can also in-clude instruction and support around family communication styles. For example, parents and other family members should be instructed to avoid blaming, scolding, or punishing patients for their OCD symptoms. Family member participation in treatment can be framed as one aspect of the "OCD fighting team," along with the patient and therapist. In this context, parent or sibling participation in exposure as part of reduction in accommodation behaviors is described as something that is helpful to the patient. Patients may protest at first and feel upset or angry with family members for not participating in compulsions. Parents often need support to use their own adaptive coping skills to stay calm and manage their distress at seeing their children upset. Parents can be coached on how to calmly respond to their child's distress, for example, restating the rationale for exposure, reminding the child that they are all on the same team fighting the OCD, and coaching the child to use an adaptive coping skill or tolerate their distress until it becomes easier for everyone.

In Chapter 1, we provided the example of Marcus, whose parents were accommodating his contamination fears by opening doors for him, picking things up off the floor for him, and making a different meal for him than the rest of the family. Parent work for Marcus would include psychoeducation to explain why participating in compulsions with Marcus was perpetuating the OCD cycle. The therapist can communicate an understanding that the parents were just trying to be helpful, decrease Marcus's distress, or help him move on with his day. As the parents learn the rationale for ERP, they will better understand why their accommodation behaviors had the opposite effect in the long term. Marcus's parents would learn about the coping skills that Marcus was learning, like mindfulness and cognitive restructuring, so they could support him in using these skills when needed. Most importantly, his parents would be an essential part of the exposure practice process. One or both parents would come into sessions with Marcus and his therapist to participate in an exposure by watching Marcus pick something up off the floor or open a door, without stepping in to help him, even if he felt contaminated and asked for help. The family's homework would be to continue these exposures in between sessions.

At first, Marcus might protest and plead with his parents to continue making a separate dinner for him, and this exposure could be broken down into smaller steps, where the parents start making one fewer separate item for Marcus each night until he could eat all of the same foods as the rest of his family. Marcus and his parents would ideally work out a reward plan where Marcus could earn points for each exposure he participated in at home, and his parents could earn points for each time they did not accommodate his compulsions. When the family reached a target number of points, Marcus would get to pick his favorite restaurant for the whole family to go out to eat or the movie they would watch for family movie night. This family reward plan emphasizes that the whole family is working together to fight OCD. Simultaneously, it will help Marcus agree to practice contamination exposures in front of his parents and, as part of the exposure, reduce the number of requests for help over time until, ultimately, he is able to refrain from asking for help.

With these practices, Marcus would become more skilled in managing his OCD symptoms on his own. Parent education would include how family life can adjust to interact around Marcus's strengths and other activities he enjoys, in place of the time and attention that was previously spent on OCD symptoms. Marcus's parents would learn that parental attention is a powerful reinforcer of child behavior and could then begin directing specific attention and praise to Marcus when he participates in exposures. This would additionally provide practice at directing their attention elsewhere when he participates in rituals. They also could start scheduling special time with Marcus doing an activity he enjoys in the evening, such as playing a game or reading a book together, so that Marcus has a reliable time to spend with his parents in lieu of the time spent doing compulsions together. Once this is all achieved, Marcus and his parents can gradually decrease the frequency of their sessions in the intensive program and learn what behaviors to look out for in order to prevent a return of OCD symptoms.

CHAPTER 9 TAKE-HOME POINTS

- Parents, as well as trusted family members or close friends, are often asked or compelled to participate in compulsions or anxiety-driven behaviors in order to alleviate distress for the individual with OCD, and these behaviors are just as important to address as the compulsions that the individual performs.
- Parents may adapt the home environment to avoid OCD triggers so that the triggers do not upset their children or disrupt the family routine, or they may unknowingly participate in a ritual, which then becomes a frequently repeated process. These cycles can create conflict, confusion, and high emotions within a family system, thus requiring a family component to treatment in order to optimize treatment outcome.
- Parental accommodation of, or participation in, OCD and anxiety-driven behaviors for children is borne out of parents' innate drives to protect their children from distress or harm. That said, these accomodations can worsen OCD symptoms and need to be addressed.
- Sessions with patients and family members together may facilitate communication around exposure practices, and it may be helpful for parents to join exposure sessions to observe the exposure process in action.
- Patients may protest parental involvement at first. Parents often need support to use their own adaptive coping skills to stay calm and manage their distress at seeing their children upset.

Psychoeducation

Psychoeducation is typically the first component of treatment for obsessive compulsive disorder (OCD), as well as for related conditions, often as early as the first assessment or feedback session. Psychoeducation at the start of treatment should provide an understanding of the symptoms and condition as a whole, plus the theory, rationale, and procedures associated with the recommended interventions. This chapter outlines the core concepts included in psychoeducation for OCD from an intensive exposure and response prevention (ERP) treatment perspective.

Psychoeducation provides information about OCD and common comorbid symptoms or disorders, developing a framework for patients and families to understand their experience of OCD symptoms and how these interfere in daily life. Psychoeducation also provides an understanding of the theory and rationale for exposure therapy, setting up what can be expected from treatment in both the short and long term. Empirical evidence supporting the treatment should also be reviewed in lay terms understandable by the patient and family. Psychoeducation is important because it ensures that the patient and family have a clear factual understanding of OCD and related symptoms. The goal here is to reduce anxiety, shame, stigma, and blame around the symptom presentation for patients and their families and to provide early education about the process of ERP. This education prepares patients and families that this treatment can be quite challenging and uncomfortable and simultaneously allow them to understand how it will benefit and help. A discussion of which strategies can be used to help manage and tolerate the difficult aspects of this treatment approach, as well as what behaviors may be less helpful for the treatment process, will increase the likelihood and ability of patients and families to tolerate the distress and persist in treatment despite discomfort.

WHAT TO INCLUDE IN PSYCHOEDUCATION

Psychoeducation for OCD often begins with an explanation of the concept and experience of an "obsession" and a "compulsion" and the relationship between the two (see Appendix Table A.1, "Appendix Skills Worksheets"). A review of common obsessions and compulsions may offer some comfort to patients that they are not alone in these experiences. If treatment involves a group component, two of the clear benefits of group treatment are the opportunity to hear from other children and teens who have similar symptom experiences, and for parents to hear from other parents about their observations and experiences parenting a child with OCD. The role of anxiety, fear, disgust, and/or other uncomfortable emotions in motivating compulsions is essential to review, including the sympathetic nervous system as the source of this emotional and physiological discomfort. The concept of a "false alarm" in OCD (e.g., Piacentini et al., 2007) underscores the reason why exposure therapy is helpful, in that the anxiety, fear, or other strong emotions associated with obsessions leads individuals to feel as if they are in danger or are threatened in some way. The false alarm analogy illustrates that one is not actually in danger just because there is an anxious or uncomfortable feeling, and that this feeling will likely diminish over time if tolerated and/or ignored. However, it is important for patients and families to understand that ERP often does not "feel good" (in fact, it's meant to feel "not-good"!), and that much of treatment will feel challenging, perhaps even making the anxiety associated with OCD feel stronger before it begins to diminish.

PSYCHOEDUCATION IN AN INTENSIVE TREATMENT SETTING

Many patients who enter into an intensive treatment program have been experiencing OCD symptoms for quite some time and may have tried other treatments. An explanation of intensive treatment and why this structure may be different from what they have previously tried is helpful. For example, in a traditional weekly therapy setting, patients may work hard at changing their behaviors during and/or immediately after their treatment session, but often as time passes between weekly sessions it becomes harder to resist giving into compulsions or to remember what was learned or gained in the treatment sessions. Behavior change requires consistency and is optimized by repetition as often as possible. Psychoeducation about intensive treatment can include the potential benefit of patients being supported in resisting compulsions more frequently or for more hours within a given week, which can augment the behavior change process.

The content of psychoeducation in the context of an intensive treatment program will be very similar to that which would be shared in a standard ERP treatment setting. However, psychoeducation in an intensive treatment program will include the rationale and benefits of intensive treatment, as described above. There are variations in the way psychoeducation may be offered depending on the structure of the intensive treatment program. Some programs will provide written information prior to the start of treatment, or a treatment workbook for patients and families to review and use within the treatment program. Psychoeducation can be provided in written materials and then reviewed in person, in both group and individual treatment modalities. When the intensive program has a rolling admission structure, psychoeducation may be covered at each entry point for new patients. This offers an opportunity for content to be repeated and reviewed for patients already in the program each time a new person enters treatment. This review can help with long-term memory and integration of the information. Patients who are further along in the treatment program can be asked to "teach" portions of the psychoeducation content to new members, which solidifies the teaching patient's own understanding and application of this information. Parents or other important support figures should be included in the initial psychoeducation sessions, either with the patient or in their own group or individual parent session. This provides context for understanding the disorder and its treatment and the role of family members in both the symptom presentation and treatment. It also offers the opportunity to begin to process what behavior change might look like and feel like for the patient and the family.

The following are important points to cover in an initial psychoeducation session:

1. OCD means that you are having intrusive, unwanted, often repetitive thoughts that cause anxiety, discomfort, or distress. In response to this discomfort, you do some behavior, routine, or ritual that you feel you must do in order to feel better. Whatever it is that makes you feel better is likely to be repeated the next time you have the same anxious or unwanted thought.
2. The uncomfortable feeling that you feel is your body's alarm system firing. It's called your "fight-or-flight" system, or your sympathetic nervous system, which is a very important system in our bodies that keeps us ready to respond if we are in danger. If we were actually in danger right now, our fight-or-flight system would fire so that we could run away quickly or fight off a danger to keep ourselves safe. However, when the system fires in response to a thought, but you are not actually in physical danger, then you are left with a rush of adrenaline and associated changes in your body. You may feel your heart beating faster, your breathing changing, your muscles tightening up, or you may feel hot, cold, sweaty, shaky, or dizzy. This feels uncomfortable, and our brains search for a source of danger to respond to.
3. Doing something to lessen the uncomfortable feeling or to get rid of the unwanted thought makes sense in the short term. In fact, it may feel like the most reasonable, rational response to your fear in the short term. However, in the long term, this behavior keeps the thoughts and uncomfortable feelings around because our brains believe that something bad might happen if we don't respond. So, each subsequent time that we feel uncomfortable, we will quickly repeat the behavior that made us feel better, even if it provided only a temporary feeling of relief.
4. ERP helps us tolerate our uncomfortable feelings long enough to make a different choice. By not immediately responding with compulsive behaviors to decrease distress, we learn that the feeling may lessen on

its own or that the thing we were afraid of did not come true. The more
we experience successful ERP, the more confident we will feel to repeat
it. This is one reason why intensive treatment is so helpful, because
exposures will be repeated many times throughout the week.

5. ERP is usually difficult and can sometimes make us feel a little worse
before we feel better. But your therapist will help you break certain
situations into smaller steps that feel more manageable for you and help
you work your way up to the most difficult or scary compulsions to
change.

CHAPTER 10 TAKE-HOME POINTS

- Psychoeducation at the start of treatment should provide an
understanding of the symptoms and condition as a whole, plus the
theory, rationale, and procedures associated with the recommended
interventions.
- Psychoeducation provides information about OCD and common
comorbid symptoms or disorders, developing a framework for patients
and families to understand their experiences of OCD symptoms and
how these interfere in daily life.
- Psychoeducation also provides an understanding of the theory and
rationale for exposure therapy, setting up what can be expected from
treatment in both the short and long term.
- Psychoeducation about intensive treatment can include the potential
benefit of being supported in resisting compulsions more frequently or
for more hours within a given week, which can augment the behavior
change process.

The Backbone of Treatment: Exposure and Response Prevention (ERP)

When treating obsessive compulsive disorder (OCD), active and consistent implementation of exposure and response prevention (ERP) is the backbone of the treatment. Said differently, ERP is the core, most important, treatment ingredient in reducing compulsions and improving functioning. This is true in both weekly outpatient treatment and in an intensive model. In this chapter, we discuss how to practically implement ERP effectively, with a focus on the intensive treatment model.

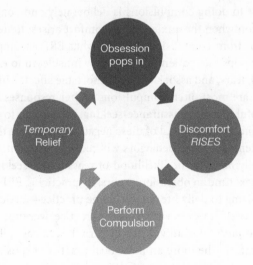

Obsessions cause anxiety or discomfort, and compulsions provide temporary relief from that anxiety or discomfort. When an individual engages in a compulsion, the discomfort goes away, which, in the moment, can seem like a positive coping skill. In reality, doing the compulsion deprives patients of the opportunity to learn what *would* have happened had they faced the fear. Further, the sensation of relief is negatively reinforcing and inadvertently teaches patients (although they are not aware that the brain is learning) that compulsions are the way to reduce obsessions and anxiety. This creates a vicious cycle where, whenever an obsession occurs, patients are "trained" to complete compulsions. While the compulsions causes temporary relief, they do not help long term, and, in fact, often cause the obsessions and compulsions to increase in severity and frequency over time.

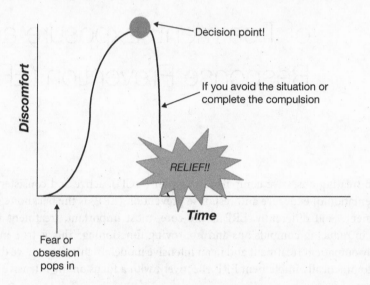

The alternative to doing compulsions is deliberately and consistently making a different decision when the anxiety or discomfort arises: to delay, modify, and ultimately refrain from compulsions. This is what ERP accomplishes: when an obsession or fear pops into patients' minds, they must learn to *expose* themselves to the obsessions, fears, and associated uncomfortable affect, while *preventing* the *responses*, which are most often compulsions. Other responses that, in the long term, are unhelpful include reassurance-seeking, attempting to neutralize or re-place thoughts, and avoidance. All of these negatively reinforce the OCD cycle by teaching the patient that these behaviors will reduce obsessions and discomfort, when they actually *increase* the likelihood of reassurance-seeking, neutralizing, or avoiding the next time an obsession occurs. By practicing ERP—first in session and then generalizing to daily life with at-home practice—anxiety or discomfort may initially increase. However, with repeated practice over time, anxiety and dis-tress will decrease *and/or* the individual will learn the critical skill of tolerating the anxiety or discomfort. The more an individual practices exposing themselves to the fear without compulsions, the more the anxiety will reduce and/or the better they will become at tolerating higher levels of anxiety.

A good analogy for this is related to working out a new muscle group at the gym. If someone goes to the gym for the first time and completes a rigorous workout (i.e., the first time someone practices ERP, even for a low-distress symptom), there will be lots of soreness and physical pain (i.e., distress) and the person may not recognize that the muscle soreness is actually teaching their body something new. If the person persists in going to the gym and working out, over time, there will be less muscle soreness, they will be able to complete more difficult exercises, and, most importantly, they will get stronger. Similarly, consistent ERP practice and willingness to tolerate emotional discomfort and obsessions increase distress tolerance over time, and, eventually, a patient will be able to complete difficult exposures and tolerate high levels of distress without doing compulsions. Use of such analogies—the working out at a gym, learning a new skill or instrument, riding a roller coaster, doing anything new for the first time—can be helpful to illustrate to patients and parents that ERP may be difficult in the short term and yet extremely helpful in the long term.

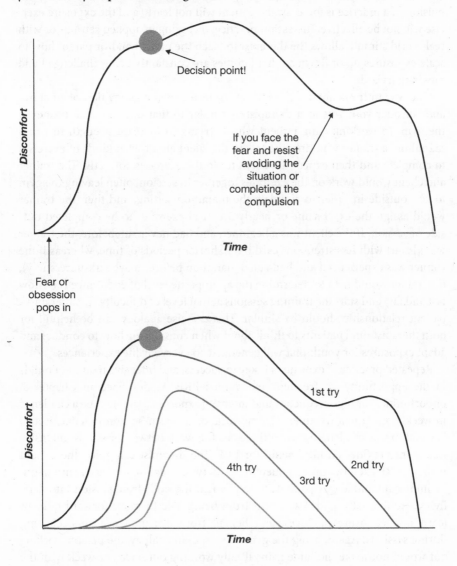

In addition to initially learning ERP in the treatment setting, ERP should be delivered in the setting in which the patient is struggling and at a level that the patient can learn. If a patient is struggling with obsessions about contamination from public transportation, the exposures should be to buses and trains, even if that means leaving the therapy room to complete the exercises. Completing exposures in the real world *within* the session itself, rather than simply using the session to discuss and assign the exposures for homework, is necessary for optimal outcomes (Franklin et al., 2011). It allows the therapist to teach, observe, and coach the patient through exposures and then to give feedback and troubleshoot.

In-session practices additionally allow the therapist to determine the right level of exposure difficulty and to model and teach how to scale exposures to the right level. If a practice is too challenging, a patient may give up and give in to a compulsion. If a practice is too easy, the patient will not learn, and the exposure exercise will not be effective. In-session practice, including in applied settings or with real-world stimuli, allows the therapist to teach the patient and/or parent how to scale exposures up or down so that families are constantly being challenged and moving forward.

One way to think about this is to return to the gym analogy described above and consider your role as a therapist as similar to that of a personal trainer at the gym. In working with a client who is trying to increase strength to run a marathon, a trainer wouldn't just *talk* to the client about what kinds of exercises to complete and then expect the client to do the exercises correctly. The trainer and client would work on the exercises together in session, often leaving the gym to run outside in order to simulate the marathon setting, and then the trainer would assign the exact same or nearly identical exercises to be completed outside of session. If the client was a beginner, and had never run before, the trainer would start with less strenuous cardio for shorter periods of time, whereas if the runner was experienced and had run a marathon before (maybe unsuccessfully), the trainer would help to determine the appropriate level of endurance (i.e., how fast and far) and start the training sessions at that level of difficulty. The therapist–patient relationship should be similar. This exercise analogy can be helpful for both therapists and patients to think about when considering how to conduct and adapt exposures for youth that will generalize to everyday life experiences.

Repeated practice of exposures is key to success, and intensive treatment builds in the opportunity for frequent and guided ERP. As described in Chapter 3, opportunities for high frequency and intensity exposures can often be a challenge in weekly outpatient treatment. Homework, or between-session practice, is also key and can be challenging when there is a full week between sessions. Intensive treatment provides an ideal setup for ERP. The therapist can guide the patient through ERP exercises on a frequent basis. Between-session practice continues to be important and allows patients to implement the skills from session into daily living. Additionally, patients benefit from being able to move forward quickly, learn new exposure practices, and benefit from live guidance and coaching during sessions. Again, using the gym or marathon analogy, the person working out would not make the same gains if only working out once per week with the trainer and would make many more gains (and more quickly too!) if engaging in workouts every day at home as prescribed by the trainer for in-between gym sessions.

Intensive treatment allows patients to engage in ERP for multiple hours a day and/or multiple times a week with a therapist. This provides an incredible opportunity to move rapidly through many exposure targets and to receive constant coaching and feedback. As discussed in Chapter 1, condensing treatment and doing *more* exposures within a short time frame may speed up the time to recovery. Patients, especially those with high levels of impairment, benefit greatly from this model. Intensive treatment can allow, in a significantly shorter time span than with weekly outpatient therapy, for return to school, functioning, and other areas of life that have been disrupted by OCD symptoms.

QUICK GUIDE ON SETTING UP EXPOSURES

Below we provide some brief tips on how to set up successful exposures. As a reminder, for therapists less experienced in the conduct of ERP, please see the references in Chapter 1 for additional treatment manuals and readings to pursue first.

1. *Set up for success!* Build a list of targets and obsessions that you and the patient will face together. Keep in mind that this does not always have to start at the easiest item and build up to the hardest, particularly as the patient progresses through treatment or for items related to significant functional impairment. We recommend using index cards for each item so that you can shuffle them up, re-rate them over time, and dive in with exposures in the area that will be most meaningful for the patient. You can always scale up or down within an item. For example, if a patient's largest area of impairment is walking without repeating steps or taking extra steps, but that is rated a 10 (on a scale from 0 to 10) when the patient begins, you still might opt to start with this item! It will allow the patient to walk fluidly again, which would make a huge impact on daily functioning. You can break the task down into smaller, more manageable challenges. Can the patient take three steps without a compulsion? How about two? Even if "walking to school without compulsions" is a 10, there may be intermediate practices that allow you to work on the most impairing target from the get-go.

2. *Practice, practice, and practice some more!* Intensive treatment allows for more ERP practice than weekly outpatient treatment. ERP is the core and most important treatment element that we want to amplify and intensify when working in an intensive model. Frequent sessions provide the opportunity for more frequent and repeated practice. These practices should translate into out-of-session settings and should also be practiced primary targets in the treatment setting itself. It

may be tempting to assign a practice for homework or to assume that "it isn't worth a full session to practice walking around the block," but remember that, if the act of walking around the block is a way to practice ERP, then completing the walk without compulsions is the most important treatment ingredient. Your patient will be learning how to do the exposures and how to prevent anxiety-driven responses and compulsions alongside you. You will be able to give feedback, enhance understanding and learning, and be a guide through these challenging practices. During exposure practices, you and the patient will be working together to titrate the difficulty level appropriately so that the patient learns to tolerate distress at the appropriate level given the patient's symptoms and stage in treatment; thus, your patient will be simultaneously practicing exposures and learning how to conduct and scale independent exposures. You will also be able to directly observe and highlight progress within sessions and across sessions when you see a patient over multiple days and multiple practices.

3. *Don't assign between-session practice that hasn't been sufficiently practiced, discussed, or approximated in sessions first!* As related to Tip 2 above, patients should know *exactly* what is expected of them between sessions for each practice assignment: How many times and for how long will they do specific exercises? Exactly what are they supposed to do, where, and with whom? Are they delaying compulsions or expected to skip compulsions entirely? To answer these questions, use the in-session practice as a guide for your patients to see that they're either expected to do the exact same thing between sessions or discuss how the in-session practice is an approximation and how the at-home practice will be different. This is why spending an hour walking around the block in session may be critical for what the patient is expected to practice at home! If there is absolutely no way to approximate the between-session practice in the therapy setting, think creatively about how it might be approximated with imaginal exposures, bringing items from home into the therapy setting or through role-plays.

4. Assign between-session practice (i.e., therapy homework), and review it at each session! As important as practicing in session is, you want to make sure that the gains are being translated outside of sessions. Homework is a great way to test this out. Can the patient complete the same exposures from session at home? What barriers came up in the home setting? Was it more (or less) challenging with you, the therapist, there? Between-session practice provides an opportunity for a patient to build mastery, show success, make progress, and uncover areas where troubleshooting is needed. In many of our intensive settings, we assign between-session practice daily, including the evenings on the same day that the patient did exposures in session, as well as weekends and days between in-person sessions. The idea here is that repeated practice in multiple settings is critical for treatment success.

SYMPTOM AND TREATMENT EXAMPLES

Intrusive Thoughts

Many children and adolescents with OCD present with intrusive thoughts. These are unwanted thoughts that the patient most often fears, is uncomfortable with, or disagrees with. For example, a child may have thoughts popping in about self-harm, even though the child does not want to engage in this behavior, and self-harming is actually the child's greatest fear. Another adolescent may have images of inappropriate sexual situations, even though these are horrifying to this teen. Many therapists struggle to identify the obsession itself when working with younger patients. With intrusive thoughts, the obsession is most often "What if this thought reflects something about me?" or "What if the content of my unwanted thoughts is true or will come true?" Associated compulsions are most often efforts to neutralize the thought in some way, such as saying "That isn't true," checking to make sure nothing bad has or will happen, or reassurance-seeking. For some patients (particularly prevalent in younger children), the obsession can involve a feeling that something "isn't right," distress or disgust about a feeling of discomfort, or a vague belief that "something bad will happen if I don't do the ritual" without an ability to describe what that "something bad" might be.

As with other symptoms, the goal in ERP is to face the obsession and fear while preventing the compulsive response. If the patient's fear is "thinking this awful thought may indicate that it is true and reflects my beliefs," then the goal would be to practice actively facing and thinking thoughts without any of the above listed common compulsions. For example, for the child who is afraid that thoughts about self-harm indicate some desire to act on them, the therapist would ask the patient to practice saying thoughts out loud, writing thoughts, and even holding a knife. For the child who fears something vaguely bad will happen or that there will be a "not just right" feeling, then the goal would be inducing and tolerating that discomfort without doing the ritual. By completing these practices over and over without any compulsions, the child will learn to face and dispel, the fear: saying a thought, thinking a thought, and even having the opportunity to act on a thought does *not* mean that it will come true. The child will also learn to tolerate (ultimately high levels of) distress when these thoughts occur.

Please note that before doing exposures to thoughts about harm, suicidal behaviors, and sexually inappropriate behaviors, it is important to complete a thorough assessment to confirm that these are truly intrusive, unwanted, ego-dystonic thoughts, rather than suicidal ideation, self-harm urges, violent urges, or sexually violent urges. If the thoughts are ego-syntonic and the patient is having thoughts about self-harm because of distress and *does* experience a true urge to engage in self-injurious behaviors, you would take a different, safety-focused course in treatment, and these thoughts would not be categorized as obsessions or treated with the above exposure exercises.

When All the Contaminants Are in the Home

Sometimes patients will present to treatment with contamination concerns, but explain that all symptoms are confined to one setting, such as the home. These patients are able to touch and interact with everything in the therapy setting and during outings, but will describe that bedroom furniture, living room couches, and other home-setting items are extremely challenging and cause severe impairment.

In these cases, it is critical to target the symptoms *when and where they cause distress*. There may be creative ways of bringing the home into the office, such as having the family bring in pillowcases and couch cushions to practice with or having the patient "contaminate" items from your office at home and then bring them back into the office to practice. If the problem still seems confined to the home environment, you may consider doing in-home sessions if that is within the scope of your practice, or utilize telehealth. As discussed in Chapter 4, telehealth has become more and more common and provides important access to situations that would otherwise be harder to access for the therapist. Using a telehealth platform, you may be able to virtually accompany a patient into a home-based room to practice contamination concerns that are specific to items in that space. It can allow you to target showering, grooming, or dressing routines that are confined to a specific area or time of day. Creativity in exposures is key: it is essential to find ways, in and out of the office, to make sure that the patient is facing the core obsessions and fears, and that the patient is tolerating distress during ERP without doing compulsions.

Troubleshooting

- What happens when a patient just won't participate?
  - Consider whether this is an issue of oppositionality, high anxiety, or a lack of understanding of the treatment model. If there is a separate concern about oppositional behavior and you learn that the patient has trouble complying with unwanted tasks, whether related to anxiety or not, you may consider and assess for oppositional defiant disorder (ODD). It is likely important to address the oppositional behavior first, and then return to OCD treatment and ERP. If, on the other hand, the oppositionality *only* arises in the context of OCD and anxiety, then it may be due to the high levels of anxiety. In this case, consider breaking down the exposure tasks into smaller units. If patients say "no!" to an exposure, teach them to consider what they *can* do, even if the steps they can take are slightly easier versions of the originally proposed exposure. It may also be helpful to return to psychoeducation as a reminder for why distress tolerance and exposures are important. External rewards that are salient to patients may also be useful.

- What if an exposure was unintentionally too difficult?
  - It is fairly common that over the course of treatment you and a patient carefully agree on and plan out an exposure, and then in the treatment setting when the patient tries the exposure, it is unexpectedly much too difficult, causes more distress than you anticipated, and the patient becomes extremely upset. As in weekly therapy, while it's never pleasant to be surprised this way, it does provide important information. After implementing coping strategies and mindfulness (*not* compulsions) to support the patient in calming down, three messages are important for the patient to hear:
    - It wasn't anyone's fault this happened.
    - The patient did a great job using adaptive coping when surprised.
    - You and the patient will, together, use these important data points to problem solve and think through whether there was anything that you might have planned differently to make the next set of exposures on target.
- It is critical that you do not stop exposures entirely for the day; otherwise, your patient may learn that avoidance is appropriate when faced with surprise or an unexpected challenging outcome. It is also critical that you and the patient think about which aspects of the exposure were too difficult: Was it just too big of a step up from the last exposure, or was it the combination of many exposures in tandem? Both of these could be addressed with subsequent exposures. Did the patient experience an obsession or start to experience increasing worry/negative emotion? In this case, mindfulness might be a more appropriate strategy to plan for if this occurs in the future.
- The patient's distress tolerance isn't improving across sessions and/or the parent reports that, following session, the patient goes home extremely upset and ends up engaging in many compulsions following an intensive session. What might be going wrong?
  - Often, children and adolescents in treatment are socially motivated and concerned about disappointing or upsetting their providers. This is especially true for those with symptoms of perfectionism or eagerness to please that are often seen in the context of generalized anxiety disorder, social anxiety disorder, and moral scrupulosity symptoms in OCD. Sometimes, these symptoms interfere with treatment such that patients agree to exposures just to "please" the therapist, despite not being ready. These patients then end up white-knuckling their way through the session. This approach is not useful for learning the graded exposure treatment model, and it may even serve as a form of flooding, which is not optimal for learning about exposures to occur. If patients or caregivers are reporting significant upset when leaving treatment regularly and/or you observe that distress tolerance isn't improving, try taking a step back to talk to the patient about the experience during exposures.

Conversely, sometimes patients engage in mental compulsions or other unobservable compulsions during exposures or after they leave the session, which serve to "neutralize" or otherwise avoid fully experiencing the distress brought on by the exposures in session. For example, prior to engaging in an exposure, a patient might internally think: "I'll just get through my session today and then wash my hands a bunch as soon as I get home." This "undoing" of exposures, even if delayed, can serve to reinforce the OCD cycle and may make symptoms worse over time. Careful discussions with your patient in advance of exposures to outline when, how, and for how long the patient should aim to practice response prevention, as well as the importance of honesty in treatment, is critical.

CHAPTER 11 TAKE-HOME POINTS

- ERP is the core, most important, treatment ingredient in reducing compulsions and improving functioning.
- By practicing ERP—first in session and then generalizing to daily life with at-home practice—anxiety or discomfort may initially increase. However, with repeated practice over time, anxiety and distress will decrease and/or the patient will learn the critical skill of tolerating the anxiety or discomfort.
- Repeated practice and exposure are key to success, and intensive treatment builds in the opportunity for frequent and guided ERP.
- Intensive treatment allows patients to engage in ERP for multiple hours a day and/or multiple times a week with a therapist.
- Creativity in exposures is key: It is essential to find ways, in and out of the office, to make sure that the patient is facing the core obsessions and fears, and that the patient is tolerating distress during ERP without doing compulsions.

Cognitive Skills
in Intensive Treatment

Learning how to shift cognitions to more realistic thought patterns is a central component of cognitive behavioral therapy (CBT). Although we recommend that treatment focus on exposure and response prevention (ERP) as the primary mode of intervention, we recognize that patients with obsessive compulsive disorder (OCD) often engage in "magical thinking," or the tendency to think that things are connected that are not. They also often experience an inflated sense of responsibility that they may cause negative events to occur that they actually have no control over. Cognitive exercises that challenge these thoughts can be a stepping stone to exposures when the exposures feel too difficult to try immediately. If a patient is able to recognize an irrational thinking pattern, it may increase willingness to engage in exposures that evoke uncomfortable feelings and thus change avoidant behavior patterns.

PRACTICAL APPLICATION OF COGNITIVE SKILLS

The core cognitive restructuring exercises teach patients to identify negative or anxious thoughts that are irrational or excessive, assess these thoughts, and consider more realistic thoughts. Identification of thoughts can be half the battle. With young children and some older adolescents, cognitive work begins by identifying a thought and distinguishing this cognition from a feeling or emotion. People often treat their thoughts as *facts*, when in reality, most thoughts reflect opinions or guesses. Introducing the concept that our thoughts or appraisals of a situation are subject to bias due to anxiety allows for the necessary next step of *shifting* distorted thoughts to more realistic ones. One way to do this is to urge patients to think about their thoughts as objectively as possible. Once the patient has identified the thought, you can have them list out evidence that supports that the thought is true, as well as evidence that indicates the thought may not be the only possibility or explanation. Encourage your patient to truly consider the facts and evidence, rather than providing statements such as "It just feels like this is true!" Once a patient has considered all the evidence for and against the thought, the next step is to come up with a different thought that is more realistic, is supported by the evidence collected, and is more helpful. You can stress to your patient that the goal is not to simply "think positively," which can sometimes be off-putting, but instead to "think *realistically*." For a sample worksheet, please see the "treatment worksheets" in the Appendix.

Another method of identifying and shifting thoughts is to review common cognitive distortions. We recommend teaching patients about cognitive distortions and going through examples of each of their own distorted thoughts and then discussing how they can shift each category to a more realistic version. The common thought distortion categories can be presented in a number of ways, and we find it helpful to have an acronym or checklist that patients can use to check their thoughts. We include a worksheet in the Appendix that lists the *Magically TINTED Thoughts*, or categories of thoughts that are distorted, or tinted, by anxiety. While magical thinking is most specific to OCD, the other *TINTED* thoughts apply both within and beyond OCD presentations. We recommend teaching these areas and going through examples of each with your patients and discuss how they can shift each category to a more realistic version.

MAGICALLY TINTED THOUGHTS

Magical *Thinking*:	This is a common distortion within OCD. Patients believe that two things are connected despite no logical connection. For example, they might worry that if they don't do a compulsion, something bad could happen to family members.
Telling the future:	Predicting the future, outcomes, or events even though the patient does not know for certain that these will come true.
Interpreting ambiguity:	Reading into vague situations and/or mind-reading what others are thinking.
Negative focus:	Zooming in on the negative aspects of a situation, while disregarding the neutral and positive aspects.
Taking blame:	Disproportionately taking blame for things that are not (exclusively) the patient's fault.
Exaggerating:	Engaging in all-or-nothing or extreme thinking, such as "This will be *terrible*," "If I got another chance it would be *perfect*," "*Everyone* hates me," or "I'm *never* going to get better."
predicting Disaster:	Catastrophizing how a situation will unfold.

In addition to cognitive restructuring exercises, cognitive coping can be a helpful skill for many patients. Coping thoughts can be "cheerleading" thoughts (e.g., "I've got this!" or "My anxiety is a false alarm, and I don't have to listen!")

that help a patient manage challenging moments, including exposures. They can also be "challenging" thoughts that combat the faulty logic, such as "You didn't do this routine last year when you didn't have OCD, and nothing bad happened, so there is no logical reason to think it is necessary now" or "Tapping three times has no logical connection to my family's safety." Cognitive coping can help patients manage challenging moments and remind them of the reality of the situation. For some patients with incessant obsessions, the process of cognitive restructuring can lead to a distressing loop of thoughts where OCD thoughts continually "outdo," "one-up," or challenge the restructured thought, in which case a prescribed cheerleading thought or already established coping thought, like "This is my OCD talking I don't have to listen" may avert this process. For a worksheet on these, see the "Getting Through Tough Exposures" worksheet in the Appendix.

While both cognitive restructuring and cognitive coping exercises can be useful to calm upset feelings associated with negative thoughts and serve as stepping stones that may pave the way to exposures, it is important to ensure that these exercises do not become a crutch, serve as safety behaviors, or even become mental compulsions. When doing exposures, patients may actively or inadvertently try to diminish the challenge by using safety behaviors. These behaviors can include relaxation exercises, subtle compulsions, and self-reassurance. Engaging in safety behaviors may make the exposure exercise feel less challenging or less real and send the message that the patient is only capable of doing the exercise *because* of the safety behavior. If used as a safety behavior, cognitive work may interfere with the patient's ability to learn to tolerate the discomfort from facing the fear stimulus or obsession head on.

MANAGING COGNITIVE SKILLS IN THE CONTEXT OF ERP

That said, there are some situations in which safety behaviors can be useful intermediate steps in exposures. For example, a patient may plan with a therapist to try an exposure with a safety behavior of saying "This is silly," as a *first step*, with the explicit plan to then move on to the goal of completing the exposure without any reassurance. This might be used as a strategic move if the target exposure was initially too challenging. Even in this case, it would be important to have the patient and family understand that you are *only* allowing a safety behavior as an intermediate step to help the patient get to the full and target exposure, and it is only a temporary allowance. Similarly, cognitive exercises might be educational. If a patient truly does not recognize that obsessions contain faulty logic, doing cognitive exercises as a preliminary step to help the patient understand the rationale for engaging in exposures can be very helpful. However, if you find yourself continually assisting a patient in restructuring obsessive thoughts in session or if you notice excessive reliance on or reciting of certain coping thoughts during exposure practices, these are clues that the cognitive exercise may be a tool for avoidance of distress and therefore should be eliminated. In some instances, the repeated practice of cognitive coping skills could become a reassurance-seeking compulsion.

Finally, for some patients, some aspects of cognitive work may be inappropriate or interfere with the treatment process. For example, some patients who are very young or have neurodevelopmental comorbidities may have difficulties with the metacognition necessary to identify obsessions or may deny obsessions and instead report disgust or distress (e.g., "It just feels gross" or "I don't know why, but I have to do the ritual"). If this is the case, it may actually be more productive to forgo restructuring exercises and instead focus solely or primarily on coping thoughts (e.g., "A thought is just a thought," "I don't have to listen even if I feel like I have to") or treating the distress as a "bully" to whom the patient responds: "You're not the boss of me; I'm in charge of what I do!"

Cognitive restructuring and cognitive coping instruction are similar in an intensive setting and in a weekly outpatient treatment. These are skills that can be taught in treatment and then infused in practices throughout treatment. Depending on the format of your program, there is a range of ways to implement and teach cognitive skills. If you run a group-based program that meets daily, you can identify a day of the week to teach or review cognitive skills. If your program is more individualized, you may opt to teach these skills early on in treatment and then return to them as needed throughout the sessions. As has been referenced previously, in a group-based program with rolling admission, veteran patients can teach the cognitive skills to newer patients, which may help in consolidating their understanding and demonstrating mastery of the techniques. While cognitive work is a core element of CBT, intensive treatment does not rely on a significant increase in cognitive practice. The additional hours per week should be spent focused on ERP, and cognitive skills can support this work.

If a patient seems to need cognitive work as a primary intervention, it may be an indicator that OCD is not the primary focus. For example, when treating generalized anxiety disorder (GAD) or major depressive disorder (MDD), there is a heavier focus on cognitive interventions. If the GAD or MDD symptoms require more intervention or attention, consider pausing the OCD treatment to address these domains with other CBT skills and then return to OCD-specific treatment when the patient is ready.

CHAPTER 12 TAKE-HOME POINTS

- Learning how to shift cognitions to more realistic thought patterns is a central component of CBT.
- Cognitive restructuring and cognitive coping instruction is similar in an intensive setting and in a weekly outpatient treatment.
- While both cognitive restructuring and cognitive coping exercises can be useful to calm upset feelings associated with negative thoughts and serve as stepping stones that may pave the way to exposures, it is important

to ensure that these thoughts do not become a crutch, serve as safety behaviors, or even become a mental compulsions.

- While cognitive work is a core element of CBT, intensive treatment does not rely on a significant increase in cognitive practice. The additional hours per week should be spent focused on ERP, and cognitive skills can support this work.

Other Skills: Relaxation/ Mindfulness

Chapter 11 discussed exposure and response prevention (ERP), the backbone of evidence-based treatment for obsessive compulsive disorder (OCD). In this chapter, we discuss some *supplemental* skills that may be helpful to use as an *augmentation* to ERP: relaxation and mindfulness. First, relaxation strategies and activities are briefly described, and we refer readers to other *Treatments That Work* manuals containing in-depth information about implementation of relaxation (e.g., *Brief Behavior Therapy for Anxiety and Depression in Youth*, Weersing et al., 2021; *Mastery of Your Anxiety and Panic*, (Barlow & Craske, 2006). We then turn to mindfulness as an attentional, experiential, and/or behavioral approach related to obsessions, with some examples of experiential mindfulness exercises. Again, if, as a therapist, you do not have prior experience with mindfulness, we urge you to consider additional trainings or readings to ensure that your understanding of and ability to implement these skills are strong, particularly so that you can provide guidance and support to patients as they may have misperceptions about the skills and their use. It will additionally allow you to correct misconceptions, answer questions, and identify when patients may be using these skills as safety behaviors and/or compulsions.

As a reminder, the relaxation and mindfulness skills presented in this chapter are considered *supplemental* or *augmentation* strategies for ERP, and, as discussed in Chapter 11, ERP is the necessary and core treatment ingredient for which the majority of treatment time should be spent. Said differently, these skills should not be applied as the sole or primary treatment component. There is currently no evidence that either relaxation and/or mindfulness is appropriate or sufficient as a stand-alone treatment for pediatric OCD. However, there is early and growing evidence, and our collective anecdotal experiences suggest, that these skills may be helpful in several ways for kids and teens participating in ERP:

- These skills may help patients feel that they have agency and can manage distress outside of treatment, particularly for symptoms that haven't yet been targeted in ERP or when triggered in the real world.

- These skills can be applied if the patient becomes more distressed in session than expected during planned ERP activities (e.g., an exposure that the therapist and patient selected because they thought it would be appropriate turns out to be too difficult on the first attempt).
- These skills can be helpful in early phases of treatment when patients are distressed often in sessions and at home, and it may be difficult for them to even disclose symptoms.
- These skills can be taught to the primary caregiver or family members participating in treatment so that all members of the family are learning and practicing skills together. This can be especially helpful for family members who are involved in compulsions and later in treatment would be expected to reduce accommodation as part of ERP practice and/or for caregivers who experience distress when they observe their child in distress.

INTRODUCING AND USING RELAXATION AND MINDFULNESS SKILLS

Typically, we recommend beginning the introduction of relaxation and mindfulness concepts and activities immediately after psychoeducation (described in Chapter 10) and prior to building the exposure hierarchy or doing cognitive work (Chapter 11). As described above, early use of these skills may be helpful for patients who are highly distressed much of the day, including during the first few weeks of treatment, as well as those for whom *disclosing* symptoms is distressing. We then recommend that therapists return to and reinforce these skills throughout sessions when ERP becomes the primary treatment focus. In fact, in our intensive work with patients, we complete mindfulness practice in many of the intensive sessions, often during "breaks" from ERP or to start or end the treatment day. In group settings with rolling admissions, veteran patients often can lead relaxation and mindfulness sessions for the group (with appropriate supervision and guidance from the therapist), which allows them to further build mastery in understanding and implementing concepts.

Relaxation

As in other cognitive behavioral therapy (CBT) interventions for anxiety and OCD, the goal of relaxation is to reduce physiological reactivity or somatic distress. In CBT manuals for anxiety (e.g., *Treatments that Work: Managing Your Anxiety and Panic*, "Chapter 6, Breathing Skills," Barlow & Craske, 2006; *Treatments that Work: Brief Behavior Therapy for Anxiety and Depression in Youth*, "Chapter 2, Relax Your Self and World," Weersing et al., 2021), discussion of these skills is typically initiated with information about the fight-or-flight response or anxiety sensitivity or when patients otherwise experience physiological and somatic symptoms as part of their symptom presentation. For example, relaxation may be introduced by first discussing that all people feel stress in different ways, that many of us feel stress in our bodies (e.g., stomachaches, tenseness in shoulders), and then turn to a discussion of where, when, and how patients feel stress in their bodies. For patients with somatic symptoms that are or can be directly linked to their OCD symptoms or when generally anxious, the discussion can also focus on how physical feelings in the body are often linked to upsetting/distressing thoughts.

In treating pediatric OCD in the intensive context, relaxation may be particularly helpful during the above-described list of situations (e.g., in early sessions when disclosing symptoms that are difficult to discuss; during out-of-session or unanticipated distress). Relaxation can also be helpful to address non-OCD symptoms, such as anger, sleep difficulty, and family conflict (whether related to the OCD or not).

The two types of relaxation that can be taught to patients and families in either individual or group formats are deep breathing and progressive muscle relaxation (PMR). Each is briefly described below, and we refer therapists to the other resources above if they have not previously learned and used these skills with patients. It should be conveyed to the patient and family that in order for these skills to be effective, they require practice even when a person is calm so that they can be successfully used when a person is distressed. We often use a sports- or performance-related analogy: a person couldn't expect to play basketball on a major team without having practiced many, many times before trying out for the team.

Although both deep breathing and PMR should be taught and practiced for at least a couple of weeks, patients often prefer one of the strategies over the other. Thus, we recommend teaching both skills and asking the patient to practice both for a week or two, and then, if one strategy is preferred over the other, the patient has a choice in selecting the one that feels most useful. The between-session practice of these skills early in treatment might occur first thing in the morning or in bed before turning off the light, assuming that the patient does not experience OCD-related distress during this time. The goal is to select a time that the patient will practice these skills consistently for a week or two *while not feeling stressed.* The easiest way to encourage this might be to assign this practice along with other treatment-related between-session assignments.

Deep breathing is meant to slow and regulate breathing (including to reduce the likelihood that a patient hyperventilates). The goal during deep breathing is to ensure that patients breathe from the diaphragm *slowly, but not so slowly that it's uncomfortable or they feel they are holding their breath* and consistently (e.g., counting 10 or 20 breaths). You may ask the patient to place one hand under the collarbone and the other on the belly button and try to regulate breathing by feeling the bottom hand (over the belly button) move up and down as the stomach fills with and then expels air, with a goal of the top hand (under the collarbone) not moving as much. Conversely, the patient may lie back on the floor or on a couch and place a book over the belly button, practicing breathing and watching the book move up and down. The most important things that patients should learn during deep breathing are that we can regulate our breath by focusing on it, and that if we try to slow the breath it may help us to feel physically calm over time. Relatedly, it may be important to convey that it takes 10 or 20 breaths (rather than one or a just a handful of breaths) to begin to feel calm in the body.

Progressive muscle relaxation is meant to address the muscle tension associated with physiological arousal during distress. This skill can be particularly helpful for patients who have tension headaches and/or stomachaches and also for caregivers who carry their stress in their shoulders, back, and/or face. PMR involves deliberate and systematic tensing and relaxing of muscle groups one set at a time (e.g., forehead, shoulders, fists, stomach, legs, toes) and noticing the distinction between the feelings of tension and relaxation. Thus, you may teach patients to start with their forehead, nose, and jaw and work their way down toward their toes, or vice versa. Conversely, you and the patient may pick a handful of body parts (fists, biceps, stomach, toes). The important components of this strategy are to *tense and then relax one body part at a time*. You may count up to five while tensing each body part as you lead the patient through the exercise and ask your patient to identify what the tense feelings feel like in that part of the body compared to the relaxed feelings. Again, patients should not tense so much that they feel pain or discomfort, but just enough that they have a strong sense of what tension feels like and, in contrast, what relaxed muscles feel like.

Together, breathing and PMR can be helpful in providing short-term or momentary feelings of calm or physical comfort. It is very important to be aware that there are explicit times when relaxation should *not* be used because it would "defeat the purpose" of ERP. For example, and as discussed in Chapter 11, exposures are meant to cause distress so that patients ultimately learn that (a) they can tolerate upset feelings and (b) that compulsions are *not* necessary when they experience obsessions and/or distress. Therefore, when exposures lead to the level of distress that the therapist and patient have discussed and anticipated during exposure planning, relaxation should not be used in the middle of, or immediately after, exposures. This is because practicing distress tolerance is critical. Using relaxation during planned exposures when the patient's level of distress is anticipated by both the therapist and the patient is *contrary* to the idea of distress tolerance; this would send a message that relaxation is important, helpful, or necessary to manage distress during exposures. It is critical to discuss this, and when to, versus when not to, use relaxation with patients and caregivers.

Relatedly, and especially if relaxation exercises are used incorrectly, patients may believe that they *must* do relaxation in order to calm down, feel relief, and/or feel less distressed. For some patients, relaxation may subsequently become a compulsion. Check in with your patients regularly about when and how they use this skill, with reminders that the goal of ERP is to deliberately tolerate increasing levels of distress without trying to compensate or minimize negative emotions. Thus, use of relaxation is a balancing act. Relaxation may be encouraged early in treatment for symptoms that haven't yet been targeted and cause significant distress in the patient's daily life and then discouraged over the course of treatment as those symptoms are actively addressed with ERP.

Mindfulness

Increasingly, third-wave approaches such as mindfulness have received empirical support as augmentation interventions for anxiety disorders and a variety of other mental health problems (e.g., Hayes et al., 2004). Some third-wave approaches focus exclusively on mindfulness as the primary intervention skill (e.g., mindfulness-based stress reduction), while others incorporate mindfulness into a larger intervention (e.g., dialectical behavior therapy; acceptance and commitment therapy). In the context of intensive treatment for pediatric patients with OCD, we recommend use of mindfulness as a single skill/practice, rather than using a full mindfulness-based intervention, with a variety of experiential exercises that can be incorporated into ERP. Unlike relaxation, which aims to reduce physiological reactivity and/or somatic distress, the purpose of mindfulness in OCD treatment is *not to increase feelings of calm or relaxation. Instead, the goal of mindfulness is to help the patient learn, and eventually recognize, that in-the-moment thoughts and feelings of distress are subjective, temporary experiences that do not always reflect reality and, for this reason, do not always require a response.* This approach encourages and assumes that, over time, patients will learn that they can tolerate distress associated with obsessions *without* engaging in compulsions. Indeed, we often use mantras in treatment (e.g., "A thought is just a thought," "No thought or feeling lasts forever," and "I can let my thought be and don't have to respond even if I'm upset") to summarize the mindful perspective in responding to obsessions or distress.

Mindfulness can be applied throughout treatment, although it may be particularly helpful during the situations described at the start of this chapter (e.g., early in treatment to return to concepts in subsequent sessions; in response to real-world OCD triggers that have not yet been addressed with ERP; for parent distress). In addition, mindfulness may be particularly useful as a means to redirect back to task when patients become distracted in session. Finally, we view experiential mindfulness practice as an excellent way to start and end the treatment day or as a scheduled break between exposure practice.

In the following sections, we describe how mindfulness concepts can be broadly applied to symptoms and then specifically utilized during experiential mindfulness practices.

APPLICATION OF MINDFULNESS TENETS TO OCD BROADLY

Mindfulness includes three core concepts: (1) paying attention, (2) to the present moment, (3) without judgment. In the context of OCD, "paying attention" typically refers to noticing or redirecting attention, "to the present moment" refers to the experiential mindfulness exercise or real-world environmental context, and "without judgment" refers to the mindfulness concept of decentering, or noticing one's thoughts without attaching emotional valence to them. Although these ideas may seem complex, they are actually quite simple to explain and implement with patients and caregivers. For example, if you and your patient are practicing the mindfulness activity of anchoring to breath (described below), your patient will be paying attention to the in-breaths and out-breaths, redirecting attention back to the breath even when other thoughts pop in, such as "I'm hungry; I wonder what's for dinner," and simultaneously refraining from self-judgement when other thoughts occur (e.g., instead of deciding, "I'm doing a bad job at this mindfulness practice," thinking "It's harder to redirect back to task today, let me try to get back to focusing on my breath"). The ultimate goal with these three mindfulness concepts is for patients to be able to identify when they are experiencing distress, anxiety, or disgust or are upset about obsessions and being able to "let go" of or redirect away from these sticky thoughts *without* trying to change, neutralize, or respond to them with compulsions.

Outside of explicit mindfulness practice, the three mindfulness concepts can also be applied in response to obsessions and distress during ERP or when obsessions are triggered in the patient's daily life. For example, when working with a patient with contamination obsessions and washing/cleaning compulsions, the therapist and patient may be practicing exposures related to touching common surfaces, such as a table and chair, and then eating candy with "dirty" hands. During exposures, the patient may report feeling extremely afraid and distressed. In response, you might prompt the patient to, not only describe the purpose of exposures and how they might help with response prevention in the long-term (as is typical in ERP), but also apply the tenets of mindfulness. For example, "Hmm, I'm hearing a judgment thought when you say you feel like you can't handle distress. What does mindfulness tell us about upsetting feelings?" or, "Has feeling scared about contamination ever lasted forever for you? Even when you were sleeping and playing video games and having fun with friends?" and "Let's take a mindful approach to these exposures. Why are we doing these exposures and what should we be paying attention to?" When your patient responds indicating that the goal of exposures is distress tolerance and not doing compulsions, you can reply: "OK! So we're paying attention to what we're doing right now, which is the exposure exercise, and you're supposed to be feeling upset. You're doing a great job! How can we try to think about the gross and scared feelings you're experiencing without you judging yourself?" Here, some of the mindfulness imagery, such as noticing thoughts as if they were leaves on a stream, clouds floating through the sky, or suitcases on a conveyor belt at the airport may be helpful. Importantly, the goal of mindfulness is to identify and experience, but not try to change, feelings of distress. Thus, mindfulness is entirely consistent with the goals of ERP.

Additionally, mindfulness can be broadly applied in response to obsessions and distress outside of explicit exposure practice in the patient's daily life. For example, patients may experience thought–action fusion related to aggressive obsessions and believe that if they have obsessions about hitting someone, it's just as bad as actually hitting someone. If the patient is early in treatment, exposures may be focused on one specific aspect of this symptom cluster (e.g., focused on a primary caregiver), though patients may experience obsessions about harming others anytime they are in the vicinity of other family members, neighbors, and peers. In this case, teaching mindfulness early can allow patients to then apply the broad mindfulness concepts to the harm-related obsessions at home during meals with siblings, when taking a walk around the neighborhood and seeing neighbors, and any other time they see someone about whom they have obsessions who is not yet the target of ERP exercises.

Thus, mindfulness can be applied with these theoretical concepts and mantras. The exercises can also be paired with a thought suppression exercise (e.g., "Don't think about a white polar bear") to demonstrate that when we try to suppress thoughts, we end up thinking about the thoughts more! Given that most children and adolescents struggle with these relatively abstract mindfulness concepts initially, we strongly encourage application with experiential mindfulness practice, both in session and during at-home practice. This experiential practice should be as concrete as possible, particularly for younger patients, in order to solidify the more theoretical concepts described above. Below we provide a variety of sample experiential mindfulness exercises, although, again, we encourage clinicians with less experience incorporating mindfulness into exposure-based treatment to pursue additional readings, trainings, and consultation.

Sample experiential mindfulness exercises. Below is a list of a few mindfulness exercises that we have found particularly helpful in the intensive treatment setting with patients. These exercises have been adapted and draw from other existing literatures, including dialectical behavior therapy and acceptance and commitment therapy. For additional detail regarding the implementation of these exercises, we refer the reader to other *Treatments That Work* and *Programs That Work* manuals that include specific exercises.

- Basic breath mindfulness, sometimes called anchoring and redirecting back to breath. Here the goal is to notice the breath *without trying to change it* (which is different from trying to slow down breathing, as in relaxation/deep-breathing exercises).
- STOP: Stop (what you're doing), Take a Breath, Observe (what's going on in the real world around you, not your thoughts or feelings), Proceed (with whatever you are supposed to be doing at that time).
- Savoring while eating a raisin or piece of chocolate, walking mindfulness, or music scribble mindfulness, where the goal is to direct (and redirect) attention to the task at hand. This type of activity can also help patients learn that they can refrain from doing something they really want to or feel they must do (e.g., holding a chocolate chip on the tongue and letting it melt, noticing the flavors, without trying to chew it, even though it tastes delicious). During and following this exercise, you might

      draw parallels between the patient's ability to refrain from doing things they really want to do to and your confidence that they can also refrain from engaging in compulsions even though they may feel like they want or have to.

- Ice cube exercise, where patients hold an ice cube in their palm without attempting to melt it (e.g., leaving the hand open), experiencing the distress and discomfort. This exercise can be both a reminder that we can tolerate distress *and* be an example that the distress dissipates on its own without us having to do anything (e.g., after a while, the ice cube melts). Many patients from our own intensive programs value this activity in particular because they are able to relate the specific example of the ice cube melting on its own to the idea that their upsetting thoughts/feelings will eventually go away if you wait long enough. Some patients even respond well to assigning this exercise at home: When patients experience obsessions related to symptoms that have not yet been targeted in treatment, they'll grab an ice cube or ask their parents for one and wait out the discomfort, with many reporting that this helps them to delay and/or refrain from compulsions.

- 54321: This exercise involves 5 things you can see, 4 things you can feel, 3 things you can hear, 2 things you can smell, and 1 thing you can taste. Although this can be done as a stand-alone exercise, it might also be useful to set a phone alarm or timer to go off randomly during exposure sessions, agreeing with patients beforehand that when the timer goes off, they will immediately redirect and do 54321 and then continue with exposures. This can help to further clarify what redirection is and how it can be used to practice mindfulness and also ultimately refrain from compulsions.

In our experience, many individuals (therapists and patients alike!) have misperceptions about mindfulness and its goals. To this end, below we provide some tips and troubleshooting related to the mindfulness tenets and experiential practice.

- Mindfulness is *not* about being calm or getting rid of upset feelings. Sometimes people *can* feel less stressed after an activity like mindful breathing, but not every time, and not for everyone. A goal of mindfulness is to notice when we're having upsetting thoughts without judging the thoughts or ourselves and then gently redirect back to whatever we're supposed to be doing.

- Mindfulness is *not* about emptying one's mind of thoughts, distracting ourselves from thoughts, or trying to get rid of thoughts. Our minds are thinking things all the time! If we try to push thoughts away, we end up thinking about them even more, like with the white polar bear (thought suppression) exercise. Instead, a goal of mindfulness is to get better at letting thoughts be without trying to change them. Here, it might also be helpful to refer to leaves on a stream, clouds in the sky, or suitcases on a conveyor belt to illustrate the idea of observing without being able to change what we're observing.

- The incorporation of mindfulness into OCD treatment is secular or unrelated to any religion or religious practice.
- Mindfulness is different from cognitive restructuring, and, in fact, the two approaches can be viewed as contradictory. In cognitive work, patients learn to challenge irrational thoughts or unlikely worries by coming up with rationales, such as alternate interpretations of fears, or estimating that risk for the outcome is low. Cognitive restructuring involves explicit attempts to change thoughts. In contrast, mindfulness involves noticing upsetting thoughts and feelings without judgment and sitting with that discomfort *without trying to change how we think and feel.*

Finally, as with relaxation, the purpose of mindfulness during exposures is not to reduce planned and anticipated distress. As described previously, mindfulness concepts *can* and *should* be used during exposures to remind ourselves that our goal is to feel distress and to refrain from trying to push it away, that we can tolerate distress, and that eventually distress will dissipate on its own without us having to try and intervene ourselves.

CHAPTER 13 TAKE-HOME POINTS

- Relaxation and mindfulness skills are considered supplemental or augmentation strategies for ERP, which is the necessary and core treatment ingredient for which the majority of treatment time should be spent.
- The goal of relaxation is to reduce physiological reactivity or somatic distress.
- The purpose of mindfulness in OCD treatment is *not* to increase feelings of calm or relaxation. Instead, the goal is to recognize that in-the-moment distressing thoughts and feelings are subjective, temporary experiences that do not always reflect reality and, for this reason, do not always require a response.

Other Skills: Problem Solving and Relapse Prevention

This chapter details two additional skills and treatment components: *problem solving* and *relapse prevention*. Problem solving may be used at any point in treatment, including during the assessment process. It can be included as a single strategy within another treatment component (e.g., problem solving during negotiation of the next exposure) or as a stand-alone 30- to 40-minute treatment technique in which patients are taught a framework so that they might conduct problem solving on their own for either obsessive compulsive disorder (OCD) or non-OCD symptoms (e.g., concerns about return to school that are not OCD related but are due to participation in intensive treatment). For some children and adolescents who have great success and motivation for treatment, problem solving may be used minimally. In contrast to problem solving, relapse prevention should be conducted with every single patient and family in anticipation of the transition out of intensive treatment.

PROBLEM SOLVING

The problem solving skill may be useful in a variety of situations, several of which are described below. Regardless of the situation, and whether the clinician is utilizing the problem solving framework themselves or directly teaching it to youth for their subsequent use, problem solving includes core steps (SOLVE: State the problem, Option generation, Look at each option, Vote!, Evaluate):

1. *State the problem.* While this seems simple and obvious, it is an
   important step. Defining *why* the problem is a problem, breaking it down
   into manageable goals, and determining how a patient will know when
   the goals have been met are important aspects of this step. Without it,
   patients may have trouble identifying the area to target or lose sight of a
   specific goal.

2. *Option generation.* This is the brainstorming stage, in which patients will come up with *many* solutions. It is important to push beyond the "go-to" solutions that children and adolescents may already have, as these go-to solutions have often been tried and have not effectively solved the problem. We encourage patients to come up with as many as 10 solutions, without judgment or evaluation at this stage. Including solutions that patients currently use (e.g., avoidance, compulsions) may also be useful because applying Step 3 below (looking at the pros/cons of each option) may help them to recognize that their current behaviors may not be helping them long term.

3. *Look at each option.* Here, patients finally have the opportunity to judge and evaluate the results of the brainstorming session. They should consider the pros and cons of each proposed solution and recognize that there is often no perfect answer: Seemingly "good" solutions have cons, and seemingly "poor" solutions have pros.

4. *Vote!* Whether completing problem solving as a group exercise or individually, it is important to elect the best possible solution of the options brainstormed. Despite there being no perfect solution, opting and committing to attempting one is important. In this step, patients should make very concrete plans about how they will implement the solutions they have elected.

5. *Evaluate.* This is the time to see if the elected option worked! At this stage, encourage patients to evaluate whether or not the solution was successful and, if it wasn't, encourage them to revisit the remaining options that they generated in Step 2. It should be noted that use of problem solving might be an iterative process: Most problems aren't solved with a single solution, and sometimes multiple solutions applied sequentially or concurrently are required.

Problem solving is important for children and adolescents in treatment and can be implemented into day-to-day life and challenges. Problem solving can also move treatment forward. It may help to identify and resolve challenges and barriers in treatment that might be related to patient symptoms, problems relating to family accommodation or functioning, and difficulty negotiating exposure hierarchy or exposure practice. It can be implemented in the moment, when these problems arise, such as when patients are afraid to talk about symptoms, or to help negotiate resistance or parent–child conflict about treatment content. Problem solving can help manage expectations for between-session practice, help patients to ask for support, or allow patients to more effectively translate in-session skills to daily living. It can also be used as a more formal exercise, in which patients take a step back to reflect on a specific challenge, and plan solutions for the future.

Even when implementing problem solving in a less formal manner, we recommend using simple and concrete language that links back to the steps listed previously in this chapter to help patients and families see how problem solving can be helpful, such as the following:

- "It sounds like this is really hard right now. What skills can we use to reduce stress in talking about this? What exactly is getting in the way, and what do you want to achieve?" (**State the problem**)
- "What are some ways we can deal with this problem?" (**Option generation**)
- "What are some benefits or downsides of each of those ideas?" (**Looking at options**)
- "Sounds like you have a lot of ideas, even if none feel perfect. What will we try?" (**Vote!**)

When taking a step back and reflecting on how to use problem solving, it can be useful to teach patients the problem solving model to work on any specific problem. Like the SOLVE model proposed here, many manuals provide acronyms to teach patients this skill. These acronyms and concrete steps may be especially helpful for situations that are not directly related to core treatment aspects of the patient's OCD symptoms but may still affect or be affected by OCD. For example, if a patient's symptoms have reduced and it is time to prepare for a return to school, the patient may be concerned about what to say or do if peers or teachers ask questions. Problem solving with role-plays can help to prepare for these types of challenges. Similarly, patients may feel unprepared to step down to outpatient care. Using the problem solving framework to isolate their worries can then help them make plans to address them. We have provided a problem solving worksheet in the Appendix.

RELAPSE PREVENTION

In some ways, relapse prevention delivered in an intensive model is not very different from relapse prevention for outpatient OCD treatment. It occurs near the end of treatment and focuses on how to carry the skills from active treatment forward. In an intensive setting, relapse prevention helps ensure that the patient feels ready to continue using skills and face challenges when transitioning to a care setting with less support. Infusing conversations about relapse prevention and termination throughout treatment will increase the chances of success as the end of treatment approaches.

While the conversation should start early, a formal relapse prevention session toward the end of treatment can provide a set of plans to prepare the family for the change or termination of intensive treatment, increase the likelihood that gains are maintained, and ensure that families know how to return to services or notify a provider if they start to notice a return of symptoms. As described in detail in Chapter 7, prior to reviewing the specific components of relapse prevention, tapering intensive treatment for several sessions or even a couple of weeks prior to discharge can be extremely helpful in identifying challenges that the family might have as they step down to outpatient care and also prepare them for the lower level of support. Relatedly, a firm handoff between intensive and outpatient treatment providers, and even having patients role-play how they would describe their treatment successes, challenges, and what they're still working on with the outpatient provider will increase the likelihood that the transition is seamless. In fact, we often recommend that patients bring their "intensive treatment binder" or documents with hierarchies, symptom tracking, worksheets, and parental monitoring to their first few outpatient appointments to aid them in describing specific exposures and skills that were helpful during their participation in intensive treatment. We provide a worksheet you can use in the Appendix.

When you, the therapist, conduct a relapse prevention session, it is critical to ask questions rather than provide didactic content, which allows the patient to lead the conversation. Your patients will be expected to remember this information on their own once they leave intensive treatment, and the relapse prevention session should serve as practice for that independent knowledge recall. We also encourage that, no matter the patient's age, parents be included in a portion of the session so that the child or adolescent can reiterate what was discussed and the parent can contribute praise and reflections. Families can often identify ways that the patient might catch early signs that symptoms might be worsening in the future. It may also be useful for the patient to document the below components of the relapse prevention discussion into a plan that can be referred to and used in the future:

1. *A comparison of the patient's symptoms and functional impairments at the start of treatment versus current symptoms and functional impairment.* Symptom monitors, such as the Children's Yale Brown Obsessive Compulsive Scale (CYBOCS) can be a very useful tool in showing patients and families how far they have come. An initial hierarchy that you created with your patient can also show how many things that used to be difficult are now highly manageable. This may also provide an opportunity to discuss what symptoms remain and how to apply the current skills to remaining focus areas.

2. *A concrete skills list.* Identify all the skills that the patient has learned and practiced and inquire about when and how patients might continue to use each skill throughout the transition from intensive treatment. The key point to emphasize when reviewing skills is that, despite distress and obsessions, the patient was able to take action and utilize skills, such as exposure and mindfulness, in order to change behavior and ultimately create change in daily living (e.g., functioning, distress). This is another opportunity for praise, reinforcement, and encouragement. Similarly, patients may also enjoy creating a list of all the activities they can do without engaging in compulsions now, which they can adapt from their exposure hierarchy.

3. *Identification of challenges and hurdles.* Have an honest discussion of situations or settings that pose challenges in your patient's home, school, and social life related to symptoms. Identifying these situations and how to manage them when the patient and family won't have such intensive

support in treatment will set them up for success. Discuss what patients and families anticipate will arise, how they will use skills to manage these challenges, and who they can turn to for support when needed.

4. *Generalization of skills to new situations and symptoms.* OCD symptoms can morph and shift over time, and even if the originally identified symptoms are well managed, ensure that your patient knows how to tackle new situations and symptoms, even hypothetically. We recommend role-playing. Have your patient play the role of therapist and pose a new set of symptoms. If you are in a group setting, you can have fellow group members pose challenges to the target patient. Have the patient practice creating a hierarchy, discussing exposures, and considering other skills to tackle the new symptoms. This exercise will allow you to assess if your patient has generalized the skills learned and whether the patient will be able to apply them more independently.

5. *Education about the course of OCD.* Discuss the difference between a *lapse* and a *relapse.* Set expectations so that the patient and family don't get discouraged by minor setbacks and instead feel empowered to use skills, and, simultaneously, make sure that the patient and family know when it might be time to reach out for help or return to a higher level of care.

CHAPTER 14 TAKE-HOME POINTS

- Problem solving may be used at any point in treatment.
- Relapse prevention should be conducted with every single patient and family in anticipation of the transition out of intensive treatment.
- Relapse prevention delivered in an intensive model is not very different from relapse prevention for outpatient OCD treatment. It always occurs near the end of treatment and focuses on how to carry the skills from active treatment forward. That said, infusing conversations about relapse prevention and termination throughout treatment will increase the chances of success as the end of treatment approaches.

While this chapter concludes Section III, the specifics of treatment elements that are used in intensive treatment, we intend that this book can be used as a reference guide. Skip around between the various sections and chapters to help with individual aspects of your program. The Appendix, which follows directly after this, provides worksheets that can be used or adapted in your treatment context and has some additional tables and information to supplement what you have read thus far. We hope you enjoy providing and engaging in intensive treatment, which can be an incredibly rewarding, robust, and effective way to treat pediatric OCD.

- Treatment Worksheets

- OCD Home-Based Symptom Assessment

- Tables

What Is OCD?

Obsessive   **=**   Obsessions are the *thoughts, images, urges, or feelings* that come in over and over, and over, and over . . .

Compulsive   **=**   Compulsions are the *behaviors* that you engage in (or things that you avoid!) to quiet those thoughts or to make yourself feel better.

Disorder   **=**   Many people have some compulsions, and even more people have obsessions! What makes it a "disorder" is when the obsessions and compulsions are messing up things in your life.

Myths and Facts About OCD

MYTHS	FACTS	Learn some more!
Anxiety and Obsessions are the WORST!!	*Actually, we NEED some anxiety, and in certain situations anxiety can help us!*	Anxiety and fear serve as our body's defense system and our emotions alert us to danger. If we are actually in danger, fear is what causes us to go into "flight-ir-flight" mode and helps us react appropriately. When we have OCD our defence system is TOO sensitive, and it goes into "danger-mode" even when there s no true danger.
Treatment will get rid of them.		CBT and ERP will teach you how to tell the difference, and how to handle situations better. Our goal is to LOWER your anxiety and to teach you how to MANAGE it better when it does come up.
I'm the only one struggling with this!	*1%–2% of kids and teenagers have OCD. MANY more have anxiety, too.*	Think of the number of people in you school. Next: Take 2% of that. Let's say you have 500 people in your school. That means about 2%, or 10 people, have OCD as well!
It is so weird!		And if we are including anxiety disorders, bring that number up to 20%, or 100 people!! It is a lot more than you might have thought.
I have a thought or image that pops into my head a lot.	*These types of thoughts are called "intrusive thoughgts" and don't necessarily relate to what you belive.*	As humans, we have TONS of thoughts every day, and many of them are strange and unimportant. OCD can make our thoughts much "stickier" and we pay more attention to them. We start saying "STOP THINKING THAT!" or "If you're thinking it. it must mean that you want or believe it!"
On some level I must believe it, or it says something about me.		The more we try NOT to think about something, the more it pops into our heads. Let's test it: try your hardest NOT to think about blue giraffes. Try harder! What are you thinking about? Probably blue giraffes. The more that you try to get rid of thoughts, the more it will pop in. ERP can help!

Thoughts

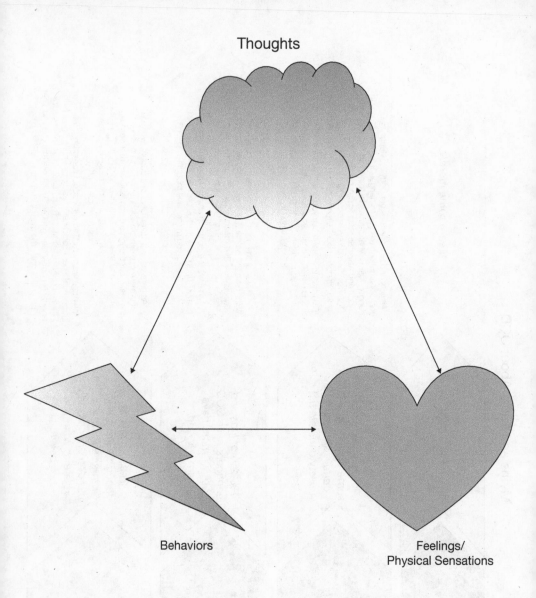

Behaviors

Feelings/
Physical Sensations

Every experience has these three components, and each influences the other.

Think of a situation.

Write out what you were thinking, feeling, and how you were behaving.
Trace how each element impacted the others.

The Obsessive Compulsive Cycle

Obsession pops in

Discomfort *RISES*

Perform Compulsion

***Temporary* Relief**

EXPOSURE WITH RESPONSE PREVENTION (ERP):

Part 1: Giving in to avoidance and compulsions

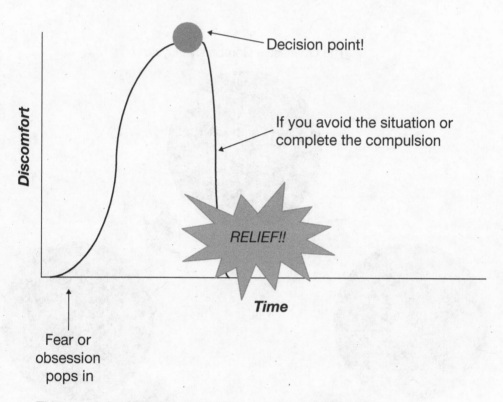

This graph looks appealing! What is wrong with it??

1) That "relief" is a reward to our bodies and brains and teaches us to do more and more compulsions or to keep avoiding.

2) We never get the chance to learn what would happen if we faced our fears, and our minds ASSUME that our anxious or OCD thoughts are correct!

"But what is the alternative? If I didn't do this, I think I would feel worse and worse until I did a compulsion!"

...See part 2!

EXPOSURE WITH RESPONSE PREVENTION (ERP):

Part 2: RESISTING avoidance and compulsions

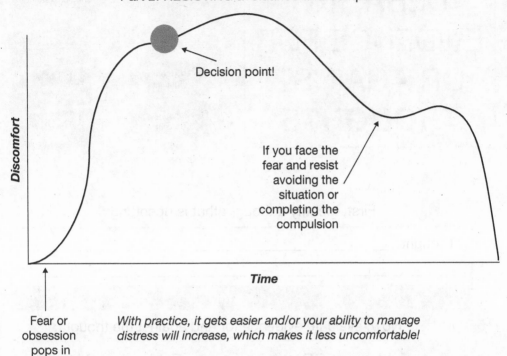

Discomfort

Decision point!

If you face the fear and resist avoiding the situation or completing the compulsion

Time

Fear or obsession pops in

With practice, it gets easier and/or your ability to manage distress will increase, which makes it less uncomfortable!

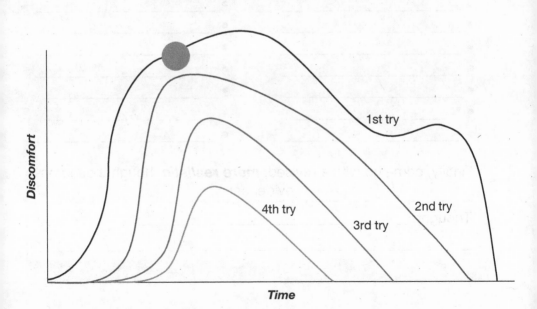

Discomfort

1st try

4th try

3rd try

2nd try

Time

DEBATING EVIDENCE FOR OR AGAINST *THOUGHTS*

Is my thought 100% true?

Perhaps it has some holes I should examine!

Fact Supporting My Thought

Fact Supporting My Thought

Fact that means my thought may not be fully accurate!

Fact that means my thought may not be fully accurate!

Fact that means my thought may not be fully accurate!

First, identify a thought that is upsetting:

Thought: _____

_____

Now, evaluate evidence for and against the thought:

Evidence FOR	Evidence AGAINST
• _____	• _____
• _____	• _____
• _____	• _____
• _____	• _____
• _____	• _____
• _____	• _____
• _____	• _____

Finally, come up with a revised, *more realistic* thought based on evidence:

Thought: _____

_____

Magically TINTED Thoughts

When we are feeling anxious, we tend to see the world a little differently. Feeling anxious can *magically* change our outlook, and it is if we are seeing the world through **TINTED** lenses. Our thoughts become a bit distorted. It is like looking wearing dark sunglasses, but not realizing that they are on!

With OCD, almost everyone has some level of **MAGICAL** thinking:

Magical Thinking	• We believe things are related that are actually not. • For example, we think that if we don't do one thing (such as a compulsion!) something bad might happen to someone we care about. • Even when we can logically see that these things are not connected, it feels as if they are.

and many of our thoughts may be TINTED

Telling the Future	• Predicting the future when you don't truly know what will happen. • It FEELS like you know exactly how something will turn out, but you are not a fortune-teller!
Intepreting Ambiguity	• Reading into situations that are unclear, or mind-reading. • When someone walks by and doesn't say hello, what might you think? Would your mind jump to "they are mad at me!"? Some situations are ambiguous, and you don't know what someone is thinking.
Negative Focus	• Zooming in on the negative aspects of a sitation. • Imagine you're at a party, and it is going well—tasty food, good music, fun people. Two hours in, someone says something mean. You tend to focus on just those 5 minutes, rather than the rest of the evening.
Taking Blame	• Disproportionately taking blame, even when it isn't your fault. • It is hard not to be extra hard on yourself.
Exaggerating	• Seeing things in an exaggerated way, or engaging in extreme thinking. • Some examples of extreme thinking: It will be TERRIBLE. It will go PERFECTLY. EVERYONE hates me. I'm NEVER going to get better. Things are often not as all-or-nothing as they seem.
predicting **D**ISASTER!!	• Catastophizing a situation. • We often think about the worst-case scenario, and how it will ruin your life forever.

Getting Through Tough Exposures:

The work we do here is hard!
You need some friends fighting for you.

Coping Thoughts:

These are your CHEER SQUAD! What would you tell a close friend who was going through some thing hard to keep them going? How would you cheer on a friend running a hard race?

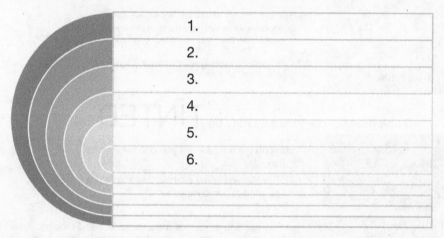

1.
2.
3.
4.
5.
6.

Challenging Thoughts:

These are your LAWYERS! They are fighting for you using facts and evidence. They are going to fight your OCD and anxious thoughts by disproving them.

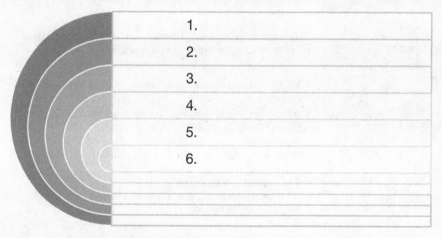

1.
2.
3.
4.
5.
6.

Relaxation Rating Sheet

Relaxation exercises can be helpful in managing stress and distress.
Provide ratings and reflections on what has been helpful for you when
you have completed these exercises.

STRESS LEVEL BEFORE	EXERCISE	STRESS LEVEL AFTER	REFLECTIONS	NOTES FOR NEXT TIME
5	Muscle relaxation	3	I became aware that I hold most of my tension in my fists!	This felt funny at first, but has been helpful the more I've practiced.
10	Deep breathing	7	When I started, I was taking BIG shallow breaths, and I felt worse. The more I practiced, the deeper my breathing got, and the better I felt.	I need to practice making sure my chest stays still and my belly moves up and down.

Mindfulness Rating Sheet

Mindfulness exercises can help you stay in the present moment. Remember—this isn't necessarily supposed to relax you. It is supposed to help you feel more aware. Provide ratings and reflections on what has been helpful for you when you have completed these exercises.

TIME OF DAY AND SITUATION	EXERCISE	REFLECTIONS	NOTES FOR NEXT TIME
After school, doing homework, thoughts were spinning	Mindfulness: Observing thoughts	It was challenging for me to complete this exercise because I was so stressed! But it did make me more aware of my thoughts, and that I don't have to change them.	Try doing some relaxation to calm down next time, and THEN use mindfulness!

SOLVE THOSE PROBLEMS!

State the Problem

- This one might feel obvious, but it is one of the most important steps! Identify a SOLVABLE problem and make sure you know exactly how you'll know if you have achieved your goal. You might need to break down a big problem into a bunch of smaller ones.
- _____
  _____

Options

- List out TEN different options! At this point, don't judge them or disregard anything. This is the time to brainstorm without shooting any option down.
- 1)
- 2)
- 3)
- 4)
- 5)
- 6)
- 7)
- 8)
- 9)
- 10)

Look closely

- List at least 2 pros and 2 cons for each option. Remember–even the best-sounding solutions have cons, and even the worst-sounding ones probably have some pros.
- 1)
- 2)
- 3)
- 4)
- 5)
- 6)
- 7)
- 8)
- 9)
- 10)

Vote!

- Elect which option you think will be the best for you after looking at the pros and cons of each one.
- _____
  _____

Evaluate

- Did your choice work? If not, go back and elect another option!

BECOMING YOUR OWN THERAPIST

What were the most helpful skills that you have learned here?

_____

_____

Thinking about your everyday life, when will you continue to practice these skills?

_____

_____

What are some things that you want to continue working on?

_____

_____

How will you continue working on future challenges? What skills will you use?

_____

_____

What are some warning signs that your OCD symptoms are creeping back in? How can you fight them?

_____

_____

What do you look back on, that seems EASY now, but was *super* hard when you started this program?

_____

_____

What exposures are you most proud of? What do you think your family or therapist was most proud of?

_____

_____

What do you know now that you WISH you had known when you started?

_____

_____

What is your favorite or funniest memory from being here?

_____

_____

My Practice Ladder

Write out a bunch of situations that are currently hard for you. In the "Day 1" column, rate how hard it would be to do (0–10). As you practice, provide new ratings in the subsequent columns.

	Day 1: Date:	Day: Date:	Day: Date:	Day: Date:	Day: Date:	Day: Date:	Day: Date:

OCD HOME-BASED SYMPTOM ASSESSMENT

The OCD Home-Based Symptom Assessment is a checklist that mimics the Children's Yale Brown Obsessive Compulsive Scale (CYBOCS) in that a youth or parent can check off areas/items of the home that may be involved in compulsions, trigger obsessions, and/or where symptoms occur. Unlike the CYBOCS, however, there is no scoring system for this measure; it is a qualitative checklist that the clinician and family can use at the start of treatment to identify domains in which symptoms occur for future exposures and throughout treatment to track progress and ensure generalization. We do encourage that if an item below is involved in a symptom but not indicated in the checklist (e.g., electronics are listed under checking compulsions in the checklist, but the youth washes/cleans electronics) the client/parent completing the checklist can write a brief note on the side of the page to indicate how the item on the checklist is related to OCD symptoms.

OCD HOME-BASED SYMPTOM ASSESSMENT

Bergman and Rozenman

This questionnaire is to be completed by parents and youth independently. Think about the places in your home in which the youth has difficulty due to OCD. Check off all that apply.

Current   **Past**

Home Entrance

_____ _____ Repeatedly entering to get a certain feeling or for any reason (please explain)

_____ _____ Repeatedly entering a specific number of times

_____ _____ Walking through it while thinking a specific thought

_____ _____ Avoiding touching the door handle or door frame

_____ _____ Repeatedly checking to ensure the door has been properly closed or locked

_____ _____ Specific rituals immediately before or after crossing the threshold into or out of your home

_____ _____ Rituals related to the light switch at the home entrance

_____ _____ Specific rituals related to the removal of shoes or clothes on entering the house

_____ _____ Other (Describe): _____

Living Room/Common Areas
Areas contaminated or need to be protected from contamination:

_____ _____ Furniture (e.g., couch, chairs, seating areas, tables, bookshelves, etc.)

_____ _____ Floor

_____ _____ Electronics (e.g., video game system, television, etc.)

_____ _____ Light switches

_____ _____ Television remote/video game controller

_____ _____ Other (Describe): _____

Checking rituals:

_____ _____ Light switches

_____ _____ Electronics

_____ _____ Other (Describe): _____

Current	Past	

Other rituals associated with this area:

		Related to numbers associated with volume or channel on television
_____	_____	Related to sitting in this area in specific positions
_____	_____	Other (Describe): _____

Kitchen
Areas contaminated or need to be protected from contamination:

		Kitchen counter
_____	_____	Sink
_____	_____	Cleaning products
_____	_____	Dishes/glasses/utensils
_____	_____	Drawers/cupboards
_____	_____	Furniture (e.g., table, chairs)
_____	_____	Appliances (Describe): _____
_____	_____	Floor
_____	_____	Light switches
_____	_____	Garbage bin
_____	_____	Other (Describe): _____

Items/areas that need to be avoided for fear of causing harm:

		Knives or knife drawer
_____	_____	Microwave (radiation)
_____	_____	Appliances (e.g., being electrocuted or cut)
_____	_____	Cleaning products/chemicals
_____	_____	Other (Describe): _____

Items/areas that need to be checked for fear of causing an accident or being wasteful?

		Faucet
_____	_____	Appliances causing fire (e.g., stove, oven, toaster, etc.)
_____	_____	Refrigerator
_____	_____	Light switches
_____	_____	Other (Describe): _____

Current	Past	
		Other rituals:
_____	_____	Needing to sit in a specific chair at the dining table
_____	_____	Needing to place items a specific way (e.g., dishes/utensils in dishwasher/cupboard, items in refrigerator)
_____	_____	Other (Describe): _____

Bathroom
Areas contaminated or need to be protected from contamination:

Current	Past	
_____	_____	Door/knob
_____	_____	Toilet
_____	_____	Bath/items in bath (List): _____
_____	_____	Shower/items in shower (List):_____
_____	_____	Sink
_____	_____	Under sink
_____	_____	Floor
_____	_____	Trash bin
_____	_____	Toilet paper roll
_____	_____	Towels
_____	_____	Toothbrush
_____	_____	Toiletries (e.g., soap, toothpaste, shampoo, etc.)
_____	_____	Light switches

Items/areas that need to be avoided for fear of causing harm:

Current	Past	
_____	_____	Pills in medicine cabinet
_____	_____	Household cleaners under sink
_____	_____	Other (Describe): _____

Items/areas that need to be checked for fear of causing an accident or being wasteful?

Current	Past	
_____	_____	Light switches
_____	_____	Appliances causing flooding (e.g., sink, shower, bath)
_____	_____	Toilet (e.g., lid, handle)
_____	_____	Light switches
_____	_____	Other (Describe): _____

Doe these rituals occur in other bathrooms? Yes: _____ No: _____

Current	Past

Garage
Areas contaminated or need to be protected from contamination:

_____ _____ Floor

_____ _____ Home entrance

_____ _____ Garage door

_____ _____ Storage areas

_____ _____ Car(s)

_____ _____ Light switches

_____ _____ Other (Describe):_____

Items/areas that need to be avoided for fear of causing harm:

_____ _____ Tools

_____ _____ Other (Describe):_____

Checking rituals:

_____ _____ Light switches

_____ _____ Locks

_____ _____ Other (Describe) _____

Laundry Area
Areas contaminated or need to be protected from contamination:

_____ _____ Floor

_____ _____ Door

_____ _____ Washer/dryer/sink

_____ _____ Hamper (e.g., used clothes, clean clothes, etc.)

_____ _____ Cleaning supplies (e.g., detergent, softener, etc.)

_____ _____ Trash bin

_____ _____ Light switches

_____ _____ Other (Describe): _____

Current	Past

Laundry Area
Checking rituals:

_____ _____ Light switches

_____ _____ Washer/dryer to ensure it is off

_____ _____ Checking related to clothes (e.g., making sure certain clothes are not washed with other clothes)

_____ _____ Locks

_____ _____ Other (Describe): _____

Your Bedroom
Areas contaminated or need to be protected from contamination:

_____ _____ Floor

_____ _____ Bed/sheets and pillows

_____ _____ Furniture (e.g., nightstand, desk, chair, dresser, etc.)

_____ _____ Closet

_____ _____ Trash bin

_____ _____ Appliances (e.g., toys, electronics, etc.)

_____ _____ Light switches

_____ _____ Other (Describe): _____

Checking rituals:

_____ _____ Light switches

_____ _____ Electronics

_____ _____ Locks

_____ _____ Other (Describe): _____

Do these rituals occur in other bedrooms? Yes: _____ No: _____

Do these rituals occur in other rooms? Yes: _____ No: _____

Do these rituals occur in other home areas? Yes: _____ No: _____

List any areas not already addressed in this form and whether they are avoided, protected, checked, or used in any compulsive behaviors: _____

TABLES

Appendix Table A.1 LIST OF COMMON OCD SYMPTOMS AND ASSOCIATED EXPOSURE
EXERCISES

Obsession or Compulsion	Exposure and Response Prevention
Disgust/fear of contamination from germs or dirt	- Touching things that are perceived as contaminated, germy, sticky, dirty, or gross - Sharing a drink or utensil with someone - Eating something that fell on the floor - Go to the bathroom without washing afterward - Reducing shower or bathing routine
Repetitive or excessive handwashing	- Decreasing the amount of time spent or decrease incidences of handwashing - Touching something the feels contaminated, germy, sticky, dirty, or gross and refraining from or delaying washing
Ritualized showering, bathing, washing, or grooming	- Purposely mess up the ritual - Do pieces of the ritual out of order - Reduce time spent on the ritual
Lucky or unlucky numbers, colors, words	- Say the unlucky word - Wear the unlucky color - Do things an unlucky number of times
Preference for odd or even numbers	- Do things an odd number of times if evens are preferred - Set TV or car volume to a challenging number
Preference for symmetry	- Create uneven piles of books or other items - Touch something on one side of the body without touching the other side - Tilt picture frames off center - Write in a way that is not even, neat, or symmetrical
Obsessive need to know something	- Avoid looking something up and tolerate the not knowing - Have family/friends practice whispering and not repeating what they have said

(*continued*)

Obsession or Compulsion	Exposure and Response Prevention
Aggressive, ego-dystonic thoughts of causing harm to someone else	- Do not avoid or "neutralize" these thoughts - Write the thought down on paper - Say the thought out loud
Intrusive, unwanted, ego-dystonic thoughts of harming self	- Hold a knife to wrist or neck without inflicting any pain or injury - Say the feared thought out loud
Hoarding or saving things you don't need	- Throw things away - Delete old posts
Preoccupation with religion or morality	- Skip a religious ritual or decrease prayers to an amount consistent with family members or congregation - Violate a rigid self-imposed rule even if it feels wrong
Checking (doors are locked, stove is off, homework is perfect)	- Resist checking - Close door once and leave - Submit homework right after completing the first time
Rereading or rewriting	- Continue reading even if unsure - Do not erase or rewrite - Purposely leave a mistake - Read quickly or skim material without going back
Mental compulsions	- Mix yourself up to interfere with the ability to complete the mental compulsion: - Count backward in your head - Recite a simple song
Intrusive, unwanted thoughts about sex, nudity, homosexuality, or other sexual topics	- Look at pictures of bathing suit models - Watch age-appropriate romantic scenes in TV shows or movies that include content similar to the thoughts - Say/repeat feared thought out loud

Appendix Table A.2 STUDIES INCLUDING CHILD AND ADOLESCENT INTENSIVE TREATMENT PROGRAMS, DIVIDED BY TYPE OF STUDY

note: This table spans multiple pages and is divided by type of study: Meta-analysis, Randomized Controlled Trial (RCT), Non-RCT Studies, Treatment Descriptions, Case Studies and Series, and Research Utilizing Intensive Treatment Programs as the Sample. Within each of these sections, the studies are listed in chronological order, starting with the most recent.

Year	Author	Title of Article	Type of Intensive Treatment	Sample
		Meta-analysis		
2015	Jónsson et al.	"Intensive Cognitive Behavioral Therapy for Obsessive-Compulsive Disorder: A Systematic Review and Meta-analysis"	Multiple trials included.	646 Children, Adolescents, & Adults
		Randomized Controlled Trial (RCT)		
2007	Storch, Geffken, et al.	"Family-Based Cognitive-Behavioral Therapy for Pediatric Obsessive-Compulsive Disorder: Comparison of Intensive and Weekly Approaches"	14 daily sessions.	40 Children & Adolescents
		Non-RCT Studies		
2020	Sperling et al.	"The Impact of Intensive Treatment for Pediatric Anxiety and Obsessive-Compulsive Disorder on Daily Functioning"	Minimum of 4 days per week for a minimum of 4 weeks, with option of extending. Group-based treatment program.	212 Children & Adolescents
2018	Whiteside et al.	"Increasing Availability of Exposure Therapy Through Intensive Group Treatment for Childhood Anxiety and OCD"	Five-day group treatment; nine 90- to 12-minute group sessions and one 30-minute individual appointment.	143 Children & Adolescents

(continued)

Appendix Table A.2 CONTINUED

Year	Author	Title of Article	Type of Intensive Treatment	Sample
2016	Farrell, Sluis, et al.	"Intensive Treatment of Pediatric OCD: The Case of Sarah"	Two 3-hour sessions across 2 weeks with e-therapy maintenance.	10 Children & Adolescents
2016	Kay et al.	"Outcome of Multidisciplinary, CBT-Focused Treatment for Pediatric OCD"	Daily 2- to 3-hour sessions in residential treatment.	72 Children & Adolescents
2016	Leonard et al.	"Residential Treatment Outcomes for Adolescents With Obsessive-Compulsive Disorder"	26.5 hours per week in residential treatment.	172 Adolescents
2016	Riise et al.	"Concentrated Exposure and Response Prevention for Adolescents With Obsessive-Compulsive Disorder: An Effectiveness Study"	Four-day groups (15 total hours); 1 post-treatment session.	22 Children & Adolescents
2014	Rudy et al.	"Predictors of Treatment Response to Intensive Cognitive-Behavioral Therapy for Pediatric Obsessive-Compulsive Disorder"	14 sessions of family-based intensive treatment over 3 weeks.	78 Children & Adolescents
2014	Whiteside et al.	"A Baseline Controlled Examination of a 5-Day Intensive Treatment for Pediatric Obsessive-Compulsive Disorder"	Five-day intensive outpatient (ten 50-minute sessions).	22 Children
2010	Storch, Lehmkuhl, et al.	"An Open Trial of Intensive Family Based Cognitive-Behavioral Therapy in Youth With Obsessive-Compulsive Disorder Who Are Medication Partial Responders or Nonresponders"	14 sessions of 90-minute family-based CBT over 3 weeks.	30 Children & Adolescents

2010	Whiteside & Jacobsen	"An Uncontrolled Examination of a 5-Day Intensive Treatment for Pediatric OCD"	5-day intensive (ten 50-minute sessions).	15 Children & Adolescents
2008	Björgvinsson et al.	"Treatment Outcome for Adolescent Obsessive-Compulsive Disorder in a Specialized Hospital Setting"	90-minute daily sessions; 60-minute self-directed sessions three times a week in hospital setting.	23 Children & Adolescents
1998	Franklin et al.	"Cognitive-Behavioral Treatment of Pediatric Obsessive-Compulsive Disorder: An Open Clinical Trial"	18 sessions over 1. month	14 Children & Adolescents
		Treatment Descriptions		
2009	Albano	"Special Series: Intensive Cognitive-Behavioral Treatments for Child and Adolescent Anxiety Disorders"	Various approaches and settings included	
2009	Marien et al.	"Intensive Family-Based Cognitive-Behavioral Therapy for Pediatric Obsessive-Compulsive Disorder: Applications for Treatment of Medication Partial- or Nonresponders"	Daily 90-minute sessions for 3 to 4 weeks	
2007	Grabill et al.	"Intensive Cognitive-Behavioral Therapy for Pediatric OCD"	Daily 90-minute sessions for approximately three weeks	
2005	Lewin et al.	"Intensive Cognitive Behavioral Therapy for Pediatric Obsessive Compulsive Disorder: A Treatment Protocol for Mental Health Providers"	Daily 90-minute sessions for approximately three weeks	

(continued)

Appendix Table A.2 CONTINUED

Year	Author	Title of Article	Type of Intensive Treatment	Sample
		Case Studies and Series		
2018	Iniesta-Sepúlveda et al.	"An Initial Case Series of Intensive Cognitive-Behavioral Therapy for Obsessive-Compulsive Disorder in Adolescents With Autism Spectrum Disorder"	24 to 80 daily sessions in partial hospitalization and intensive outpatient	9 Adolescents
2017	Le et al.	"Intensive Exposure and Response Prevention for Adolescent Body Dysmorphic Disorder With Comorbid Obsessive-Compulsive Disorder and Major Depressive Disorder"	27 sessions in five weeks	1 Adolescent
2017	Merricks et al.	"A Case Report of Intensive Exposure-Based Cognitive Behavioral Therapy for a Child With Comorbid Autism Spectrum Disorder and Obsessive-Compulsive Disorder"	Intensive treatment in the context of severe comorbidities	1 Adolescent
2016	Farrell, James, et al.	"Treatment of Comorbid Obsessive-Compulsive Disorder in Youth With ASD: The Case of Max"	Three three-hour sessions with e-therapy follow up	1 Adolescent
2016	Reid et al.	"Intensive Cognitive-Behavioral Therapy for Comorbid Misophonic and Obsessive-Compulsive Symptoms: A Systematic Case Study"	14 sessions over three weeks	1 Adolescent

2014	Ojserkis et al.	"Pediatric Obsessive-Compulsive Disorder: An Illustration of Intensive Family-Based Treatment Delivered via Web Camera"	Five day web intensive; twice daily 60 to 75 minute sessions	1 Child
2010	Pence et al.	"Intense CBT: The Effectiveness of Intensive Cognitive Behavior Therapy: A Case Study in Pediatric Obsessive Compulsive Disorder"	Daily 90-minute sessions (11 total sessions)	1 Adolescent
2008	Whiteside et al.	"Five-Day Intensive Treatment for Adolescent OCD: A Case Series"	Ten sessions over five days	3 Adolescents
2007	Storch, Bagner, et al.	"Sequential Cognitive-Behavioral Therapy for Children With Obsessive-Compulsive Disorder With an Inadequate Medication Response: A Case Series of Five Patients"	Daily 90-minute sessions for three weeks	5 Children & Adolescents
2006	Fernandez et al.	"The Principles of Extinction and Differential Reinforcement of Other Behaviors in the Intensive Cognitive-Behavioral Treatment of Primarily Obsessional Pediatric OCD"	Five consecutive in-person sessions, then five in vivo or telephone sessions	1 Adolescent
2006	Savva & Rees	"Manualised Cognitive-Behavioural Therapy in the Intensive Treatment of Adolescent Obsessive-Compulsive Disorder"	150-minute sessions over eight weeks	2 Adolescents

(continued)

Appendix Table A.2 CONTINUED

Year	Author	Title of Article	Type of Intensive Treatment	Sample
2006	Whiteside & Abramowitz	"Relapse Following Successful Intensive Treatment of Pediatric Obsessive-Compulsive Disorder: A Case Study"	14 daily therapy sessions over three weeks	1 Adolescent
2001	Franklin et al.	"Treatment of Pediatric Obsessive-Compulsive Disorder: A Case Example of Intensive Cognitive-Behavioral Therapy Involving Exposure and Ritual Prevention"	11 sessions delivered five-days a week	1 Child
Research Utilizing Intensive Treatment Programs as the Sample				
2020	Hojgaard et al.	"Predictors of Treatment Outcome for Youth Receiving Intensive Residential Treatment for Obsessive–Compulsive Disorder (OCD)"		314 Adolescents
2020	Wei et al.	"Emotion Regulation Strategy Use and Symptom Change During Intensive Treatment of Transitional Age Youth Patients With Obsessive Compulsive Disorder"		176 Adolescents and Young Adults
2020	Gregory et al.	"Cost-Effectiveness of Treatment Alternatives for Treatment-Refractory Pediatric Obsessive-Compulsive Disorder"		Hypothetical Cohort
2019	Zaboski et al.	"Quality of Life in Children and Adolescents With Obsessive-Compulsive Disorder: The Pediatric Quality of Life Enjoyment and Satisfaction Questionnaire (PQ-LES-Q)"		225 Children & Adolescents
2019	de Diaz et al.	"Sleep-Related Problems in Pediatric Obsessive-Compulsive Disorder and Intensive Exposure Therapy"		103 Children & Adolescents

Year	Author	Title	Sample
2018	Wu et al.	"Quality of Life and Burden in Caregivers of Youth With Obsessive-Compulsive Disorder Presenting for Intensive Treatment"	72 Children & Adolescents
2018	La Buissonière-Ariza et al.	Family accommodation of anxiety symptoms in youth undergoing intensive multimodal treatment for anxiety disorders and Obsessive-Compulsive Disorder: Nature, clinical correlates, and treatment response	138 Children & Adolescents
2016	Farrell, Oar, et al.	"Brief Intensive CBT for Pediatric OCD With E-Therapy Maintenance"	10 Children & Adolescents
2016	Knowles et al.	"Is Disgust Proneness Sensitive to Treatment for OCD Among Youth?: Combination of Diagnostic Specificity and Symptom Correlates"	472 Children & Adolescents
2015	Williams et al.	"Minority Participation in a Major Residential and Intensive Outpatient Program for Obsessive-Compulsive Disorder"	924 Children, Adolescents & Adults
2014	Brennan et al.	"Intensive Residential Treatment for Severe Obsessive-Compulsive Disorder: Characterizing Treatment Course and Predictors of Response"	281 Adolescents & Adults
2014	Leonard et al.	"The Effect of Depression Symptom Severity on OCD Treatment Outcome in an Adolescent Residential Sample"	126 Adolescents
2013	Selles et al.	"Prevalence and Clinical Correlates of Treatment Concerns in a Sample of Treatment Seeking Youth With Obsessive–Compulsive Disorder"	27 Children & Adolescents
2011	Olino et al.	"Evidence for Successful Implementation of Exposure and Response Prevention in a Naturalistic Group Format for Pediatric OCD"	41 Children & Adolescents

(continued)

Appendix Table A.2 CONTINUED

Year	Author	Title of Article	Type of Intensive Treatment	Sample
2010	Merlo et al.	"Cognitive Behavioral Therapy Plus Motivational Interviewing Improves Outcome for Pediatric Obsessive-Compulsive Disorder: A Preliminary Study"		16 Children & Adolescents
2010	Storch, Lewin, et al.	"Defining Treatment Response and Remission in Obsessive-Compulsive Disorder: A Signal Detection Analysis of the Children's Yale-Brown Obsessive-Compulsive Scale"		109 Children & Adolescents
2009	Storch et al.	"Children's Florida Obsessive Compulsive Inventory: Psychometric Properties and Feasibility of a Self-Report Measure of Obsessive-Compulsive Symptoms in Youth"		82 Children & Adolescents
2008	Storch, Merlo, Larson, Geffken, et al.	"Impact of Comorbidity on Cognitive-Behavioral Therapy Response in Pediatric Obsessive-Compulsive Disorder"		96 Children & Adolescents
2008	Storch, Merlo, Larson, Bloss, et al.	"Symptom Dimensions and Cognitive-Behavioural Therapy Outcome for Pediatric Obsessive-Compulsive Disorder"		92 Children & Adolescents
2006	Storch et al.	"Cognitive-Behavioral Therapy for PANDAS-Related Obsessive-Compulsive Disorder: Findings From a Preliminary Waitlist Controlled Open Trial"		7 Children & Adolescents

Abramowitz, J. S., & Ryan, J. J. (2014). Obsessive-compulsive disorder in the *DSM-5*. *Clinical Psychology: Science and Practice, 21*, 221–235.

Albano, A. M. (2009). Special series: Intensive cognitive-behavioral treatments for child and adolescent anxiety disorders. *Cognitive and Behavioral Practice, 16*(3), 358–362.

American Academy of Child and Adolescent Psychiatry. (2012). Practice parameter for the assessment and treatment of children and adolescents with obsessive-compulsive disorder. *Journal of the American Academy of Child and Adolescent Psychiatry, 51*(1), 98–113.

American Psychiatric Association. (2013). *Diagnostic and statistical manual of mental disorders* (5th ed.). Arlington, VA: American Psychiatric Association.

American Psychiatric Association, Koran, L. M., Hanna, G. L., Hollander, E., Nestadt, G., & Simpson, H. B. (2007). Practice guideline for the treatment of patients with obsessive-compulsive disorder. https://scholar.google.com/scholar?hl=en&as_sdt= 0%2C33&q=American+Psychiatric+Association%2C+Koran%2C+L.+M.%2C+ Hanna%2C+G.+L.%2C+Hollander%2C+E.%2C+Nestadt%2C+G.%2C+%26+ Simpson%2C+H.+B.+%282007%29.+Practice+guideline+for+the+treatment+of+ patients+with+obsessive-compulsive+disorder.&btnG=

Anholt, G. E., Aderka, I. M., Van Balkom, A. J. L. M., Smit, J. H., Schruers, K., Van Der Wee, N. J. A., ...Van Oppen, P. (2014). Age of onset in obsessive-compulsive disorder: Admixture analysis with a large sample. *Psychological Medicine, 44*(1), 185.

Barlow, D. H., & Craske, M. G. (2006). *Mastery of your anxiety and panic.* Oxford University Press.

Björgvinsson, T., Wetterneck, C. T., Powell, D. M., Chasson, G. S., Webb, S. A., Hart, J., ... Stanley, M. A. (2008). Treatment outcome for adolescent obsessive-compulsive disorder in a specialized hospital setting. *Journal of Psychiatric Practice, 14*(3), 137–145.

Bouton, M. E., Kenney, F. A., & Rosengard, C. (1990). State-dependent fear extinction with two benzodiazepine tranquilizers. *Behavioral Neuroscience, 104*(1), 44.

Brennan, B. P., Lee, C., Elias, J. A., Crosby, J. M., Mathes, B. M., Andre, M. C., ... Hudson, J. I. (2014). Intensive residential treatment for severe obsessive-compulsive disorder: Characterizing treatment course and predictors of response. *Journal of Psychiatric Research, 56*, 98–105.

Bustos, S. G., Maldonado, H., & Molina, V. A. (2009). Disruptive effect of midazolam on fear memory reconsolidation: Decisive influence of reactivation time span and memory age. *Neuropsychopharmacology, 34*, 446–457.

Cottraux, J. A., Bouvard, M., Claustrat, B., & Juenet, C. (1984). Abnormal dexameth-asone suppression test in primary obsessive-compulsive patients: A confirmatory report. *Psychiatry Research, 13*(2), 157–165.

de Diaz, N. A. N., Farrell, L. J., Waters, A. M., Donovan, C., & McConnell, H. W. (2019). Sleep-related problems in pediatric obsessive-compulsive disorder and intensive ex-posure therapy. *Behavior Therapy, 50*(3), 608–620.

Farrell, L. J., James, S. C., Maddox, B. B., Griffiths, D., & White, S. (2016). Treatment of comorbid obsessive-compulsive disorder in youth with ASD: The case of Max. *In Clinical handbook of obsessive-compulsive and related disorders* (pp. 337–355). Cham, Switzerland: Springer.

Farrell, L. J., Oar, E. L., Waters, A. M., McConnell, H., Tiralongo, E., Garbharran, V., & Ollendick, T. (2016). Brief intensive CBT for pediatric OCD with E-therapy mainte-nance. *Journal of Anxiety Disorders, 42*, 85–94.

Farrell, L. J., Sluis, R., & Waters, A. M. (2016). Intensive treatment of pediatric OCD: The case of Sarah. *Journal of Clinical Psychology, 72*(11), 1174–1190.

Feusner, J., Moody, T., Lai, T. M., Sheen, C., Khalsa, S., Brown, J., ... O'Neill, J. (2015). Brain connectivity and prediction of relapse after cognitive-behavioral therapy in obsessive-compulsive disorder. *Frontiers in Psychiatry, 6, 74.*

Fernandez, M. A., Storch, E. A., Lewin, A. B., Murphy, T. K., & Geffken, G. R. (2006). The principles of extinction and differential reinforcement of other behaviors in the intensive cognitive-behavioral treatment of primarily obsessional pediatric OCD. *Clinical Case Studies, 5*(6), 511–521.

Foa, E. B., Liebowitz, M. R., Kozak, M. J., Davies, S., Campeas, R., Franklin, M. E., ... Tu, X. (2005). Randomized, placebo-controlled trial of exposure and ritual preven-tion, clomipramine, and their combination in the treatment of obsessive-compulsive disorder. *American Journal of Psychiatry, 162*(1), 151–161.

Flament, M. F., Whitaker, A., Rapoport, J. L., Davies, M., Berg, C. Z., Kalikow, K., Sceery, W., & Shaffer, W. (1988). Obsessive compulsive disorder in adolescence: An epidemiological study. *Journal of the American Academy of Child and Adolescent Psychiatry, 27*, 764–771.

Franklin, M. E., Freeman, J. B., & March, J. S. (2019). *Treating OCD in children and adolescents: A cognitive behavioral approach.* New York: Guilford Press.

Franklin, M. E., Kozak, M. J., Cashman, L. A., Coles, M. E., Rheingold, A. A., & Foa, E. B. (1998). Cognitive-behavioral treatment of pediatric obsessive-compulsive disorder: An open clinical trial. *Journal of the American Academy of Child and Adolescent Psychiatry, 37*(4), 412–419.

Franklin, M. E., Sapyta, J., Freeman, J. B., Khanna, M., Compton, S., Almirall, D., ... March, J. S. (2011). Cognitive behavior therapy augmentation of pharmacotherapy in pediatric obsessive-compulsive disorder: The Pediatric OCD Treatment Study II (POTS II) randomized controlled trial. *JAMA, 306*(11), 1224–1232. https://doi.org/10.1001/jama.2011.1344

Franklin, M. E., Tolin, D. F., March, J. S., & Foa, E. B. (2001). Treatment of pediatric obsessive-compulsive disorder: A case example of intensive cognitive-behavioral therapy involving exposure and ritual prevention. *Cognitive and Behavioral Practice, 8*(4), 297–304.

Freeman, J. B., & Marrs Garcia, A. (2009). *Family based treatment for young children with OCD. Therapist guide.* New York: Oxford University Press.

Geller, D. A. (2006). Obsessive-compulsive and spectrum disorders in children and adolescents. *Psychiatric Clinics, 29*(2), 353–370.

Geller, D. A., Biederman, J., Stewart, S. E., Mullin, B., Martin, A., Spencer, T., & Faraone, S. V. (2003). Which SSRI? A meta-analysis of pharmacotherapy trials in pediatric obsessive-compulsive disorder. *American Journal of Psychiatry, 160*(11), 1919–1928.

Geller, D. A., Hoog, S. L., Heiligenstein, J. H., Ricardi, R. K., Tamura, R. O. Y., Kluszynski, S., ... Fluoxetine Pediatric OCD Study Team. (2001). Fluoxetine treatment for obsessive-compulsive disorder in children and adolescents: A placebo-controlled clinical trial. *Journal of the American Academy of Child and Adolescent Psychiatry, 40*(7), 773–779.

Geller, D. A., & March, J. (2012). Practice parameter for the assessment and treatment of children and adolescents with obsessive-compulsive disorder. *Journal of the American Academy of Child and Adolescent Psychiatry, 51*(1), 98–113.

Geller, D. A., Wagner, K. D., Emslie, G., Murphy, T., Carpenter, D. J., Wetherhold, E., ... Gardiner, C. (2004). Paroxetine treatment in children and adolescents with obsessive-compulsive disorder: A randomized, multicenter, double-blind, placebo-controlled trial. *Journal of the American Academy of Child and Adolescent Psychiatry, 43*(11), 1387–1396.

Grabill, K., Storch, E. A., & Geffken, G. R. (2007). Intensive cognitive-behavioral therapy for pediatric OCD. *Behavior Therapist, 30*(1), 19.

Gregory, S. T., Kay, B., Riemann, B. C., Goodman, W. K., & Storch, E. A. (2020). Cost-effectiveness of treatment alternatives for treatment-refractory pediatric obsessive-compulsive disorder. *Journal of Anxiety Disorders, 69,* 102151.

Hansen, B., Hagen, K., Öst, L. G., Solem, S., & Kvale, G. (2018). The Bergen 4-day OCD treatment delivered in a group setting: 12-month follow-up. *Frontiers in Psychology, 9,* 639.

Hart, G., Panayi, M. C., Harris, J. A., & Westbrook, R. F. (2014). Benzodiazepine treatment can impair or spare extinction, depending on when it is given. *Behaviour Research and Therapy, 56,* 22–29.

Hayes, S. C., Follette, V. M., & Linehan, M. (Eds.). (2004). *Mindfulness and acceptance: Expanding the cognitive-behavioral tradition.* Guilford Press.

Højgaard, D. R., Schneider, S. C., La Buissonnière-Ariza, V., Kay, B., Riemann, B. C., Jacobi, D., ... Storch, E. A. (2020). Predictors of treatment outcome for youth receiving intensive residential treatment for obsessive–compulsive disorder (OCD). *Cognitive Behaviour Therapy, 49*(4), 294–306.

Iniesta-Sepúlveda, M., Nadeau, J. M., Ramos, A., Kay, B., Riemann, B. C., & Storch, E. A. (2018). An initial case series of intensive cognitive–behavioral therapy for obsessive–compulsive disorder in adolescents with autism spectrum disorder. *Child Psychiatry & Human Development, 49*(1), 9–19.

Jenike, M. A. (1990). The pharmacological treatment of obsessive-compulsive disorders. *International Review of Psychiatry, 2*(3–4), 411–425.

Jónsson, H., Kristensen, M., & Arendt, M. (2015). Intensive cognitive behavioural therapy for obsessive-compulsive disorder: A systematic review and meta-analysis. *Journal of Obsessive-Compulsive and Related Disorders, 6,* 83–96.

Kay, B., Eken, S., Jacobi, D., Riemann, B., & Storch, E. A. (2016). Outcome of multidisciplinary, CBT-focused treatment for pediatric OCD. *General Hospital Psychiatry, 42,* 7–8.

Kessler, R. C., Berglund, P., Demler, O., Jin, R., Merikangas, K. R., & Walters, E. E. (2005). Lifetime prevalence and age-of-onset distributions of *DSM-IV* disorders in the National Comorbidity Survey Replication. *Archives of General Psychiatry, 62*, 593–602.

Kircanski, K., & Peris, T. S. (2015). Exposure and response prevention process predicts treatment outcome in youth with OCD. *Journal of Abnormal Child Psychology, 43*, 543–52. https://doi.org/10.1007/s10802014-9917-2

Knowles, K. A., Viar-Paxton, M. A., Riemann, B. C., Jacobi, D. M., & Olatunji, B. O. (2016). Is disgust proneness sensitive to treatment for OCD among youth?: Examination of diagnostic specificity and symptom correlates. *Journal of Anxiety Disorders, 44*, 47–54.

Koran, L. M., & Simpson, H. B. (2013). *Guideline watch (March 2013): Practice guideline for the treatment of patients with obsessive-compulsive disorder.* Arlington, VA: American Psychiatric Association.

La Buissonnière-Ariza, V., Schneider, S. C., Højgaard, D., Kay, B. C., Riemann, B. C., Eken, S. C., ... Storch, E. A. (2018). Family accommodation of anxiety symptoms in youth undergoing intensive multimodal treatment for anxiety disorders and obsessive-compulsive disorder: Nature, clinical correlates, and treatment response. *Comprehensive Psychiatry, 80*, 1–13.

Le, T. A. P., Merricks, K., Nadeau, J. M., Ramos, A., & Storch, E. A. (2017). Intensive exposure and response prevention for adolescent body dysmorphic disorder with comorbid obsessive–compulsive disorder and major depressive disorder. *Clinical Case Studies, 16*(6), 480–496.

Leonard, R. C., Franklin, M. E., Wetterneck, C. T., Riemann, B. C., Simpson, H. B., Kinnear, K., ... Lake, P. M. (2016). Residential treatment outcomes for adolescents with obsessive-compulsive disorder. *Psychotherapy Research, 26*(6), 727–736.

Leonard, R. C., Jacobi, D. M., Riemann, B. C., Lake, P. M., & Luhn, R. (2014). The effect of depression symptom severity on OCD treatment outcome in an adolescent residential sample. *Journal of Obsessive-Compulsive and Related Disorders, 3*(2), 95–101.

Lewin, A. B., Storch, E. A., Merlo, L. J., Adkins, J. W., Murphy, T., & Geffken, G. A. (2005). Intensive cognitive behavioral therapy for pediatric obsessive compulsive disorder: A treatment protocol for mental health providers. *Psychological Services, 2*(2), 91.

March, J. S., Biederman, J., Wolkow, R., Safferman, A., Mardekian, J., Cook, E. H., ... Wagner, K. D. (1998). Sertraline in children and adolescents with obsessive-compulsive disorder: A multicenter randomized controlled trial. *JAMA, 280*(20), 1752–1756.

Marien, W. E., Storch, E. A., Geffken, G. R., & Murphy, T. K. (2009). Intensive family-based cognitive-behavioral therapy for pediatric obsessive-compulsive disorder: Applications for treatment of medication partial- or nonresponders. *Cognitive and Behavioral Practice, 16*(3), 304–316.

Merlo, L. J., Storch, E. A., Lehmkuhl, H. D., Jacob, M. L., Murphy, T. K., Goodman, W. K., & Geffken, G. R. (2010). Cognitive behavioral therapy plus motivational interviewing improves outcome for pediatric obsessive–compulsive disorder: A preliminary study. *Cognitive Behaviour Therapy, 39*(1), 24–27.

Merricks, K. L., Nadeau, J. M., Ramos, A., & Storch, E. A. (2017). A case report of intensive exposure-based cognitive behavioral therapy for a child with comorbid autism spectrum disorder and obsessive-compulsive disorder. *Journal of Cognitive Psychotherapy, 31*(2), 118–123.

Moody, T. D., Morfini, F., Cheng, G., Sheen, C., Tadayonnejad, R., Reggente, N., ... Feusner, J. D. (2017). Mechanisms of cognitive-behavioral therapy for obsessive-compulsive disorder involve robust and extensive increases in brain network connectivity. *Translational Psychiatry, 7*(9), e1230–e1230.

Murray, C. J. L., & Lopez, A. D. (1996). *The global burden of disease: A comprehensive assessment of mortality and disability from diseases, injuries, and risk factors in 1990 and projected to 2020.* Cambridge, MA: Harvard University Press.

Ojserkis, R., Morris, B., & McKay, D. (2014). Pediatric obsessive-compulsive disorder: An illustration of intensive family-based treatment delivered via web camera. *Clinical Case Studies, 13*(1), 68–79.

Olino, T. M., Gillo, S., Rowe, D., Palermo, S., Nuhfer, E. C., Birmaher, B., & Gilbert, A. R. (2011). Evidence for successful implementation of exposure and response prevention in a naturalistic group format for pediatric OCD. *Depression and Anxiety, 28*(4), 342–348.

O'Neill, J., Gorbis, E., Feusner, J. D., Yip, J. C., Chang, S., Maidment, K. M., ... Saxena, S. (2013). Effects of intensive cognitive-behavioral therapy on cingulate neurochemistry in obsessive–compulsive disorder. *Journal of Psychiatric Research, 47*(4), 494–504.

Pence, S. L., Jr., Storch, E. A., & Geffken, G. R. (2010). Intense CBT: The effectiveness of intensive cognitive behavior therapy: A case study in pediatric obsessive compulsive disorder. *Annals of the American Psychotherapy Association, 13*(1), 58–63.

Peris, T. S., & Piacentini, J. C. (2016). *Helping families manage childhood OCD. Therapist guide.* New York: Oxford University Press.

Peris, T. S., Rozenman, M. S., Sugar, C. A., McCracken, J. T., & Piacentini, J. (2017). Targeted family intervention for complex cases of pediatric obsessive-compulsive disorder: A randomized controlled trial. *Journal of the American Academy of Child and Adolescent Psychiatry, 56*(12), 1034–1042.

Piacentini, J., Langley, A., & Roblek, T. (2007). *Cognitive behavioral treatment of childhood OCD: It's only a false alarm therapist guide.* New York: Oxford University Press.

POTS Team. (2004). Cognitive-behavior therapy, sertraline, and their combination for children and adolescents with obsessive-compulsive disorder: The Pediatric OCD Treatment Study (POTS) randomized controlled trial. *JAMA, 292*(16), 1969–1976.

Reggente, N., Moody, T. D., Morfini, F., Sheen, C., Rissman, J., O'Neill, J., & Feusner, J. D. (2018). Multivariate resting-state functional connectivity predicts response to cognitive behavioral therapy in obsessive–compulsive disorder. *Proceedings of the National Academy of Sciences of the United States of America, 115*(9), 2222–2227.

Reid, A. M., Guzick, A. G., Gernand, A., & Olsen, B. (2016). Intensive cognitive-behavioral therapy for comorbid misophonic and obsessive-compulsive symptoms: A systematic case study. *Journal of Obsessive-Compulsive and Related Disorders, 10*, 1–9.

Riddle, M. A., Reeve, E. A., Yaryura-Tobias, J. A., Yang, H. M., Claghorn, J. L., Gaffney, G., ... Walkup, J. T. (2001). Fluvoxamine for children and adolescents with obsessive-compulsive disorder: A randomized, controlled, multicenter trial. *Journal of the American Academy of Child and Adolescent Psychiatry, 40*(2), 222–229.

Riise, E. N., Kvale, G., Öst, L. G., Skjold, S. H., Hansen, H., & Hansen, B. (2016). Concentrated exposure and response prevention for adolescents with obsessive-compulsive disorder: An effectiveness study. *Journal of Obsessive-Compulsive and Related Disorders, 11*, 13–21.

Rosa-Alcázar, A. I., Sánchez-Meca, J., Gómez-Conesa, A., & Marín-Martínez, F. (2008). Psychological treatment of obsessive–compulsive disorder: A meta-analysis. *Clinical Psychology Review, 28*(8), 1310–1325.

Rudy, B. M., Lewin, A. B., Geffken, G. R., Murphy, T. K., & Storch, E. A. (2014). Predictors of treatment response to intensive cognitive-behavioral therapy for pediatric obsessive-compulsive disorder. *Psychiatry Research, 220*(1–2), 433–440.

Sánchez-Meca, J., Rosa-Alcázar, A. I., Iniesta-Sepúlveda, M., & Rosa-Alcázar, Á. (2014). Differential efficacy of cognitive-behavioral therapy and pharmacological treatments for pediatric obsessive–compulsive disorder: A meta-analysis. *Journal of Anxiety Disorders, 28*(1), 31–44.

Savva, D., & Rees, C. (2006). Manualised cognitive–behavioural therapy in the intensive treatment of adolescent obsessive–compulsive disorder. *Behaviour Change, 23*(3), 200–220.

Saxena, S., Gorbis, E., O'Neill, J., Baker, S. K., Mandelkern, M. A., Maidment, K. M., ... London, E. D. (2009). Rapid effects of brief intensive cognitive-behavioral therapy on brain glucose metabolism in obsessive-compulsive disorder. *Molecular Psychiatry, 14*(2), 197–205.

Scahill, L., Riddle, M. A., McSwiggin-Hardin, M., Ort, S. I., King, R. A., Goodman, W. K., ... Leckman, J. F. (1997). Children's Yale-Brown obsessive compulsive scale: Reliability and validity. *Journal of the American Academy of Child and Adolescent Psychiatry, 36*(6), 844–852.

Selles, R. R., Rowa, K., McCabe, R., Purdon, C., & Storch, E. A. (2013). Prevalence and clinical correlates of treatment concerns in a sample of treatment seeking youth with obsessive–compulsive disorder. *Journal of Obsessive-Compulsive and Related Disorders, 2*(3), 286–291.

Shikatani, B., Vas, S. N., Goldstein, D. A., Wilkes, C. M., Buchanan, A., Sankin, L. S., & Grant, J. E. (2016). Individualized intensive treatment for obsessive-compulsive disorder: A team approach. *Cognitive and Behavioral Practice, 23*(1), 31–39.

Silverman W. K., & Albano A. M. (1996). *The Anxiety Disorders Interview Schedule for DSM–IV—Child and parent versions*. San Antonio, TX: Psychological Corporation.

Skoog, G & Skoog, I. (1999). A 40-year follow-up of patients with obsessive-compulsive disorder. *Archives of General Psychiatry, 56*, 121–127.

Sperling, J., Boger, K., & Potter, M. (2020). The impact of intensive treatment for pediatric anxiety and obsessive-compulsive disorder on daily functioning. *Clinical Child Psychology and Psychiatry, 25*(1), 133–140.

Stein, D. J., Craske, M. A., Friedman, M. J., & Phillips, K. A. (2014). Anxiety disorders, obsessive-compulsive and related disorders, trauma-and stressor-related disorders, and dissociative disorders in *DSM-5*. *American Journal of Psychiatry, 171*(6), 611–613.

Steketee, G. (1993). Social support and treatment outcome of obsessive compulsive disorder at 9-month follow-up. *Behavioural and Cognitive Psychotherapy, 21*(2), 81–95.

Storch, E. A., Bagner, D. M., Geffken, G. R., Adkins, J. W., Murphy, T. K., & Goodman, W. K. (2007). Sequential cognitive-behavioral therapy for children with obsessive–compulsive disorder with an inadequate medication response: A case series of five patients. *Depression and Anxiety, 24*(6), 375–381.

Storch, E. A., Geffken, G. R., Merlo, L. J., Mann, G., Duke, D., Munson, M., ... Goodman, W. K. (2007). Family-based cognitive-behavioral therapy for pediatric obsessive-compulsive disorder: Comparison of intensive and weekly approaches. *Journal of the American Academy of Child and Adolescent Psychiatry, 46*(4), 469–478.

Storch, E. A., Khanna, M., Merlo, L. J., Loew, B. A., Franklin, M., Reid, J. M., ... Murphy, T. K. (2009). Children's Florida obsessive compulsive inventory: Psychometric properties and feasibility of a self-report measure of obsessive–compulsive symptoms in youth. *Child Psychiatry and Human Development, 40*(3), 467–483.

Storch, E. A., Lehmkuhl, H. D., Ricketts, E., Geffken, G. R., Marien, W., & Murphy, T. K. (2010). An open trial of intensive family based cognitive-behavioral therapy in youth with obsessive-compulsive disorder who are medication partial responders or nonresponders. *Journal of Clinical Child and Adolescent Psychology, 39*(2), 260–268.

Storch, E. A., Lewin, A. B., De Nadai, A. S., & Murphy, T. K. (2010). Defining treatment response and remission in obsessive-compulsive disorder: A signal detection analysis of the Children's Yale-Brown Obsessive Compulsive Scale. *Journal of the American Academy of Child and Adolescent Psychiatry, 49*(7), 708–717.

Storch, E. A., Merlo, L. J., Larson, M. J., Bloss, C. S., Geffken, G. R., Jacob, M. L., ... Goodman, W. K. (2008). Symptom dimensions and cognitive-behavioural therapy outcome for pediatric obsessive-compulsive disorder. *Acta Psychiatrica Scandinavica, 117*(1), 67–75.

Storch, E. A., Merlo, L. J., Larson, M. J., Geffken, G. R., Lehmkuhl, H. D., Jacob, M. L., ... Goodman, W. K. (2008). Impact of comorbidity on cognitive-behavioral therapy response in pediatric obsessive-compulsive disorder. *Journal of the American Academy of Child and Adolescent Psychiatry, 47*(5), 583–592.

Storch, E. A., Murphy, T. K., Geffken, G. R., Mann, G., Adkins, J., Merlo, L. J., ... Goodman, W. K. (2006). Cognitive-behavioral therapy for PANDAS-related obsessive-compulsive disorder: Findings from a preliminary waitlist controlled open trial. *Journal of the American Academy of Child and Adolescent Psychiatry, 45*(10), 1171–1178.

Taylor, C. J. (2016). *OCD: A workbook for clinicians, children and teens actions to beat, control & defeat obsessive compulsive disorder.* Au Claire, WI: PESI Publishing & Media.

Walkup, J. T., Albano, A. M., Piacentini, J., Birmaher, B., Compton, S. N., Sherrill, J. T., ... Kendall, P. C. (2008). Cognitive behavioral therapy, sertraline, or a combination in childhood anxiety. *New England Journal of Medicine, 359*(26), 2753–2766.

Weersing, V. R., Gonzalez, A., & Rozenman, M. (2021). *Brief Behavioral Therapy for Anxiety and Depression in Youth: Therapist Guide.* Oxford University Press.

Wei, M. A., Van Kirk, N., Reid, A. M., Garner, L. E., Krompinger, J. W., Crosby, J. M., ... Weisz, J. R. (2020). Emotion regulation strategy use and symptom change during intensive treatment of transitional age youth patients with obsessive compulsive disorder. *Journal of Behavioral and Cognitive Therapy, 30*(2), 95–102.

Whiteside, S. P., & Abramowitz, J. S. (2006). Relapse following successful intensive treatment of pediatric obsessive-compulsive disorder: A case study. *Clinical Case Studies, 5*(6), 522–540.

Whiteside, S. P., Brown, A. M., & Abramowitz, J. S. (2008). Five-day intensive treatment for adolescent OCD: A case series. *Journal of Anxiety Disorders, 22*(3), 495–504.

Whiteside, S. P., Dammann, J. E., Tiede, M. S., Biggs, B. K., & Hillson Jensen, A. (2018). Increasing availability of exposure therapy through intensive group treatment for childhood anxiety and OCD. *Behavior Modification, 42*(5), 707–728.

Whiteside, S. P., & Jacobsen, A. B. (2010). An uncontrolled examination of a 5-day intensive treatment for pediatric OCD. *Behavior Therapy, 41*(3), 414–422.

Whiteside, S. P., McKay, D., De Nadai, A. S., Tiede, M. S., Ale, C. M., & Storch, E. A. (2014). A baseline controlled examination of a 5-day intensive treatment for pediatric obsessive-compulsive disorder. *Psychiatry Research, 220*(1–2), 441–446.

Williams, M. T., Sawyer, B., Leonard, R. C., Ellsworth, M., Simms, J., & Riemann, B. C. (2015). Minority participation in a major residential and intensive outpatient program for obsessive-compulsive disorder. *Journal of Obsessive-Compulsive and Related Disorders, 5*, 67–75.

Wu, M. S., Hamblin, R., Nadeau, J., Simmons, J., Smith, A., Wilson, M., ... Storch, E. A. (2018). Quality of life and burden in caregivers of youth with obsessive-compulsive disorder presenting for intensive treatment. *Comprehensive Psychiatry, 80*, 46–56.

Zaboski, B. A., Gilbert, A., Hamblin, R., Andrews, J., Ramos, A., Nadeau, J. M., & Storch, E. A. (2019). Quality of life in children and adolescents with obsessive-compulsive disorder: The Pediatric Quality of Life Enjoyment and Satisfaction Questionnaire (PQ-LES-Q). *Bulletin of the Menninger Clinic, 83*(4), 377–397.

For the benefit of digital users, indexed terms that span two pages (e.g., 52–53) may, on occasion, appear on only one of those pages.

Tables are indicated by *t* following the page number